Pocket
Menu Reader
Greece

Déspoina Afthonídou

LANGENSCHEIDT
NEW YORK · BERLIN · MUNICH · VIENNA · ZURICH

Originally published in Italy under the title of:

HOW TO EAT OUT IN GREECE
© Gremese Editore s.r.l. – Via Virginia Agnelli
88 – 00151 Roma – Italy

English translation:
Adrian Mercieca

Cover photo:
Mauritius, Mittenwald

© 2000 by Langenscheidt Publishers,
Inc. Maspeth, N.Y. 11378
Printed in Germany

Light, sea, smells… memories of a holiday in the land of the sun: Greece. Like all countries in the Mediterranean, Greece is a favorite destination for visitors not only because of its glorious past and cultural and artistic treasures, but also for its present-day attractions, those which form part of everyday life, such as, for example, its table. Anthropologists say that gastronomy is part of a country's cultural expression. And, indeed, Greece is a prime example. In fact, the word "gastronomy," with its etymological roots that go back to ancient Greek, means "the law of the stomach." Food, how it is cooked and eaten, is a universal and essential part of all men's lives. We may all speak a myriad of different languages, but by exploring the favorite dishes of peoples around the world, here is a universal way we can all communicate and better get to know each other!

This guide will introduce you to all the typical Greek dishes and specialties as well as their origins, with suggestions on what (and how!) to order. It also includes a section of recipes of some of the tastiest dishes you may want to prepare once back home. Its aim is to help you truly become acquainted with Greek cuisine, to appreciate its qualities, to choose restaurants wisely, and to feel at ease when ordering. For, of course, what better way to build bonds between people than by having a meal together? Not knowing what to order or what is being served could be an unnecessary barrier to creating a mood of friendship, sharing, and fun!

MAIN CHARACTERISTICS OF GREEK CUISINE

Greek cuisine is based mainly upon the typical products of the Mediterranean and is therefore rich in fish, seafood, vegetables, olive oil, and herbs (particularly rosemary and oregano). However, wheat and other cereals are also common.

From a gastronomic point of view, Greece can be divided into two different regions: the islands and the mainland. The cuisine found on the islands is quite light and consists mainly of fish and seafood; on the mainland, the cuisine is equally rich in protein, though meat and vegetables make up the principal foods.

The common denominator, however, of both of these cuisines is olive oil, a basic ingredient used not only for seasoning vegetables eaten raw, but also for cooking. Oil is considered an extremely vital commodity and is abundantly used in all the regions without exception. There are many other foods that also play an important role in Greece's culinary tradition such as yoghurt. This may be served as dessert with honey from oregano, or used to prepare the sauce τζατζικι (*zah-zee-kee*; see "Sauces and Condiments") which is excellent with fried fish or vegetables. Greek yoghurt is also delicious served very simply on white rice, as πιλαφι (*pee-lah-fee*; see "National Dishes").

On the other hand, Τα μεζεδακια (*tah metz-eh-dah-kee-ah*) or ορεκτικα (*oh-rek-tee-ka*; see "Sauces and Condiments"), makes an original appetizer that is perfect, for example, served before a good σουβλακι (*soov-lah-kee*; see "National Dishes"), skewers of pork, beef or veal fillets wrapped in pita bread, πιτα, another famous specialty.

Among gastronomic highlights, fresh fish, molluscs, and shellfish are favorites everywhere in Greece and fish abounds even in the mountain regions. If you're an avid fisherman and want to cast your line off the coast of Greece, the catch will probably be excellent, since this is one of the richest parts of the Mediterranean. However, we do recommend that you let the local fishermen be your guides and, above all, that you never set out without a fishing permit from the local police. Fish is relatively expensive and, of course, prices are even higher during the summer.

Also, remember that prices shown on the menu refer to the cost *per kilo* and not to the portion.

In the mountain regions, lamb and goat meat are popular, but beef and veal are also very good. Other typical meat products are the regional cold cuts and seasoned sausages, τα σουτζου–κακια (*tah soo-zoo-<u>kah</u>-kee-ah*; see "Sausages and Cold Cuts"). Finally, concerning Greek pastries, you will discover an infinite number of delightful treats that vary from region to region: on the island of Chios, for example, orange and lemon blossoms are prepared in a thick sweet syrup; on Hydra, pastries with almond-paste filling; on Siros, in the Cyclades Islands, τα λου–κουμια (*tah loo-<u>koo</u>-mee-ah*) are made, as well as other types of pastries described in the chapter, "Pastries."

A separate section in this guide is dedicated to wines, which are excellent in Greece whether white, rosé, or red. However, we strongly recommend that you try, at least once, the famous chilled Ρετσινα (*Ret-<u>see</u>-nah*; see "Wines"). Although most of these products are distributed all over Greece, it is also nice to venture out and taste local specialties. However, as in all countries, the quality of these foods, of course, varies with the restaurant.

A LOOK AT THE HISTORY OF GREEK CUISINE AND ITS ORIGINS

The history of Greece's culinary art goes back to very distant times. Cultural change and the traditions of many different peoples influenced its development. Unfortunately, no true body of literature on the history of Greek cuisine exists. Time has destroyed many written testimonies and only one text has come down to us, the Δειπνοσοφισται (*Dip-nohs-soh-fis-teh*) which in English could be translated as "The Sophists of Food," by Atheneus. This book narrates the evolution and development of the art of Greek cuisine up to the third century B.C. Here we find the names of the most famous cooks of the classical period and the dishes they prepared. Though this is the only source we have, it is enough to establish the most important periods of Greece's culinary tradition.

The first period, from the age of Homer until the fifth century B.C., is the one for which, of course, we have the least amount of historical information.

The second period, a glorious epoch during which Greece's culinary art attained levels of great refinement, extended from the fifth century B.C. (also known as the "golden century") until the reign of Alexander the Great. We find frequent references to the great cooks of the period such as Hariadis, Thimbron, Agis, Nireus, Sotridis. Referring to them, king Nikomidis wrote, "Ουδεν μαγειρος του ποιητου διαφερει, νους γαρ εστιν εκατερω, τουτων τεχνη" or, "The cook differs in no way from the poet, for the labor of the mind prevails in both, and the fruit it bears is art."

The best cooks came from the islands of Andros and Chios. However, we should remember that the works they produced were never esteemed in an artistic sense by society and, in fact, none of these men was ever considered for admittance into the Pantheon of heroes or divinities. Over the centuries their glory went unrecognized and, moreover, during those times a head cook invariably belonged to the slave class. Aesop was an excellent example. Though he wrote poetry and cooked exquisitely for his master, he remained forever a slave. And then there was Kadmos, founder of Thebes, who worked as assistant cook in the kitchens of the King of Sidon – a man of genius, to say the least, seeing that legend has it that he was also the creator of the Greek alphabet.

The period from the third century B.C. until 1400 A.D., and most particularly during the Byzantine Empire, was the time when Greek cooking truly reached its apogee.

And, with the Crusades, it spread to Rome and throughout

the Western World. With the fall of Constantinople to the Turks, the fourth period of Greek's culinary history began and lasted until the end of the nineteenth century. At the beginning of this era, the Greek culinary arts, as well as the other arts, were perpetuated in the isolation of monasteries, only to emerge some centuries later with Greece's independence from the Ottoman Empire. Nevertheless, Turkish rule did not make itself felt so much in the Greeks' way of cooking, as in their words and expressions for food, which little by little seeped into the language of the population. For example, the ancient expression κοπτοι (*kop-tee*) that also appears in the book Δειπνοσοφισται (*Dip-noh-soh-fis-teh*), was used to mean "meat balls." This word was adopted by the Turks who changed the pronunciation into *kof-tah*, which was then modified again by the Greeks into its present form, *kef-teh*.

In places of silence and contemplation such as monasteries, however, the language, even gastronomic, remained untouched. Monasteries, even in those days, being absolutely impregnable fortresses, offered a refuge to those in danger. Many cooks in the service of the imperial court, fleeing foreign invaders, found protection in the monasteries. Even these cooks, however, were apparently obliged to don the monk's robe, mitre included. To distinguish the real monks from the the false ones, however, their caps were changed from black to white, the cap that became, and still remains today, the symbol of chefs the world over.

Also exempt from this linguistic influence (again, in terms of culinary vocabulary) were the islands; particularly those more difficult to reach. The Turkish troops did not possess a fleet equipped for conquering territories accessible only by sea. Thus even if, theoretically, the islands fell under the jurisdiction of the Ottoman Empire, in reality they were never subjected to any real physical occupation by the Turks.

INTRODUCTION

The invasions of foreign peoples created economic inequalities within Greek society. Power passed into the hands of the Turks who enjoyed lives of ease, whereas the Greek population was extremely impoverished. This situation gave rise to a large body of literature that drew upon this theme, referring to the rich meals enjoyed by the sultan in his seraglio and the poor food of the slaves who were forced to sneak into the sultan's palace for bread to feed their own children. Out of this theme also grew the legendary figure of "Karaghiozis," one of the main characters in many works written for shadow puppet theater.

The present period, from the 1800s to today, has shown a clear break with the cuisine adopted during the Ottoman Empire. Nevertheless present-day cuisine cannot be considered particularly genuine either, since many dishes have been adopted from foreign cuisine – this time, as a result of the great tourist "invasions."

THE GREEK MEAL

The traditional Greek meal is comprised of only a few courses and will often consist of two dishes and dessert. For a detailed description of these dishes, you may refer to their specific chapters in our guide. Here, we will take a quick look at only some of the best-known specialties that characterize the Greek menu.

As everywhere, the meal begins with appetizers, τα μεζεδα–κια (*tah mets-zeh-dak-yah*) or ορεκτικα (*oh-rek-tee-kah*) that may be served hot or cold.

The classic appetizer is τυροπιτακια (*tee-roh-pee-tah-kee-ah*), a puff pastry filled with cheese φετα (*feh-tah*). An alternative to *tee-roh-pee-tah-kee-ah* is κρεατοπιτακια (*kreh-ah-toh-pee-tah-kee-ah*), which has a minced meat filling instead. Other famous hors-d'oeuvres are τα ντολμαδακια (*tah dol-mah-<u>dah</u>-kee-ah*), vine-leaf rolls stuffed with rice and served cold, or the same rolls filled with minced meat and a sauce called αυγολεμονο (*av-goh-<u>leh</u>-moh-noh*), which must be served warm. Finally, there are τα κεφτεδακια (*tah kef-teh-<u>dah</u>-kee-ah*), fried meat balls. Further appetizers are vegetables, above all eggplant and zucchini, which can be fried or grilled. Appetizers are sometimes enriched with τζατζικι (*zah-<u>zee</u>-kee*), a yoghurt sauce described previously. The second course, considered the main course, usually consists of a meat or fish dish with various vegetables, γαρνιτουρες (*gar-nee-<u>too</u>-res*). There is a great variety of dishes to choose from, to suit every taste. The famous, "Greek salad," delicious and light, is called χωριατικη (*hoh-ree-<u>ah</u>-tee-kee*) and includes tomatoes, cucumber, onion, black olives, and <u>feh</u>-tah cheese, seasoned with olive oil, vinegar, and oregano. Unlike many other countries, the Greeks do not usually end their meals with cheese (but, of course, you are always free to disregard custom) before dessert. With dessert, which can be no other than μπακλαβας (*bak-lah-<u>vahs</u>*), καταϊφι (*kah-*

tah-ee-fee) or γαλακτομπουρεκο (*gah-lak-toh-boo-reh-koh*), the three most famous and typical Greek desserts, the traditional meal is complete. However, not to be forgotten are also the assorted pastries, fruit salads, ice creams (κασατο (*kas-sah-toh*) and καϊμακι (*kah-ee-mah-kee*), and fresh fruit. Among the most renowned are seedless grapes and sultana grapes, or κορινθιακη (*koh-rin-thee-ah-kee*). After dessert, as is customary in many Mediterranean countries, an after dinner liqueur follows. Generally, this is ρακι (*rah-kee*), a type of aromatic spirit still produced according to age-old methods. Because of its very pungent, dry taste, however, *rah-kee* might not always be to everyone's liking. Coffee is not usually served after meals.

In many restaurants, meals can be ordered à la carte, and in the smaller places where regional cooking is served, it is perhaps wise to ask the waiter or waitress for suggestions.

In Greece, tourists will find they can eat well almost everywhere and restaurants abound, ranging from the most elegant (and often, of course, the most expensive), to typical and more economical places. Hotels, too, usually have a restaurant for their resident and temporary guests. The standard of course varies from hotel to hotel, but in general it is quite good since these establishments, in order to meet Health Department regulations, are inspected frequently.

The average price for a meal in Greece is quite reasonable, and even inexpensive, compared to prices in other countries in Western Europe. Credit cards accepted for payment are usually displayed at the entrance of restaurants.

A word about opening hours: restaurants are normally open from noon until 3:30 P.M., and in the evening from 8:00 to midnight. Generally the same for restaurants all over Greece, these hours vary according to the season and in the summer are more flexible.

As mentioned, Greece is a Mediterranean country whose table offers an abundance of tempting dishes. Indeed, with so many inviting places to choose from, the Greeks like to say that the only thing that might stop you from sitting down in a εστιατόριο *es-tee-ah-toh-ree-oh* Greek for "restaurant" - and having a nice meal, will simply be that you won't be able to make up your mind!

In the big cities and tourist spots there are many luxurious restaurants where international chefs propose fine dishes that combine the most recent trends in modern dietetics with all the characteristics of traditional Greek cuisine. In these restaurants, some of the most prestigious wines, both domestic and foreign, are available.

You will enjoy a comfortable, elegant atmosphere, subtle decor, air conditioning, and quiet background music. We recommend you reserve a table at least a day in advance in this type of restaurant, especially during the tourist season.

For those who have a weakness for snacks, there are the Ουζερι (*oot-tseh-<u>ree</u>*) or μεζεδοπωλεια (*meh-tseh-doh-poh-<u>lee</u>-ah*) where only appetizers of all kinds, both hot and cold, are served. There are so many to choose from that they will make a meal in themselves! And all accompanied, of course, by a good l'Ουζο (<u>oo</u>-*tsoh*) aperitif, or Ρετσινα (*reh-<u>tsee</u>-nah*) wine, or cold beer, and your table will suddenly burst into a carnival of colors, tastes, and aromas: a festive display of the cook's most delicious creations. Many restaurants propose a tourist menu or fixed-price menu, but we recommend that you order à la carte.

That way, you are free to try whatever strikes your fancy, and for a similar price.

A good rule of thumb when choosing a restaurant is to look for the Greeks' own favorite places. In small towns, away from the bustling cities, it is easier to find moderately priced top-quality restaurants. Or, if your discovery of Greece's natural beauty takes you to the islands, we definitely suggest you try one of the ψαροταβερνες (*psah-roh-tah-<u>ver</u>-nes*), or

RESTAURANTS IN GREECE

"fish inns." *Psah-roh-tah-ver-nes* are also numerous in the big cities along the coast and in the small port towns near Pireus. The delicious smells of fish, meat, and vegetables frying, or being barbecued, are an irresistable invitation to taste the local cooking. The specialty offered in *psah-roh-tah-ver-nes* is fish (always fresh, of course), barbecued, after being seasoned with olive oil, lemon, and oregano.

We should also mention the "floating" *psah-roh-tah-ver-nes*, veritable pile dwellings on the sea, open exclusively during Maritime Week, the last week of June. Of course the main specialty of the floating *psah-roh-tah-ver-nes* is also fish, seafood, and shellfish. In addition, you will also find a great variety of appetizers and excellent wines on the menu. Live entertainment is often organized to make the evenings complete, in which case it is always best to reserve. The entrance price is all-inclusive and is advertised in various newspapers to avoid any surprises.

Another type of restaurant that offers live music is called τα μπουζουκια (*tah boo-tsoo-kee-ah*). This name comes from a musical instrument, the Greek guitar (though its shape is more similar to the mandoline). Even if Greek popular music is almost exclusively played in the *boo-tsoo-kee-ah*, gastronomically speaking this type of restaurant is a veritable crossroads of culinary influences. Meals are ordered à la carte or based on the waiter's suggestions. The *boo-tsoo-kee-ah* are especially famous for another feature: here is where it is traditional to break your dishes just for το κεφι (*toh keh-fee*) or, "just for the fun of it!" A truly unique experience.

Τα σουβλατζιδικα (*tah soo-vlah-zee-dee-kah*) are a type of very popular and inexpensive Greek fast food restaurant. You can order skewers of meat with πιττα (*pee-tah*) and τζατζικι (*zah-zee-kee*) sauce, for only 250 drachmas, a little over a dollar. Other economical places to eat are the τα τυρπιταδικα (*tah tee-roh-pee-tah-dee-kah*), stalls where you can have puff pastry rolls filled with φετα (_feh_-tah) right out of the oven. This is the ideal place to get a quick bite when you're in a hurry. Finally, τα τυροπιταδι-κα (_toh ex-oh-hee-kah_) are restaurants found in the countryside. Here traditional dishes and barbecued meat are mainly served.

In addition to Greek restaurants, there are also, of course, restaurants that serve foreign or specialized cuisine such as Chinese, Italian, or vegetarian.

SAUSAGES AND COLD CUTS

Not one region or island in Greece exists that is not a producer of sausages and cold cuts, almost always seasoned with spices and garlic. Nevertheless, of all the regions, it is in the North that the production of pure pork sausages is the most developed, whereas in the distant Ionian islands, pork meat may also be mixed with vegetables before being made into sausages and cold cuts.

Domestic demand is so great that exportation of these products is impossible. In fact, sausages and cold cuts are often imported into Greece to meet national consumption.

Αλλαντικα διαφορα **(Al-lan-dee-kah dee-ah-foh-rah):** Various kinds of sausages, fresh or dried, made with pork, seasoned with garlic and spices.

Λουκανικα **(Loo-kah-nee-kah):** This term refers to sausages and frankfurters made with pork meat seasoned with garlic. They are only eaten cooked.

Μορταδελλα **(Mor-tah-del-lah):** Produced in all regions, particularly in Salonika, this is a very large, cooked sausage, seasoned with garlic and pistachios. It is a pale pink cold cut meat with square pieces of fat and grains of pepper embedded in it.

Παστουρμας **(Pahs-toor-mas):** In the past, this was a sausage imported from Egypt. Compact, medium-sized, it is made from camel's meat. Now produced in Attica, in the region around Athens, the meat, seasoned with garlic, is dark red and covered with hot paprika. *Pahs-toor-mas* is also served with fried eggs and cheese.

Σαλαμι αερος **(Sah-lah-mee ah-eh-ros):** Produced in all the regions, this sausage made from pork meat has a distinctive red color and contains small pieces of fat, sometimes seasoned with garlic and pepper. It resembles Italian salami.

Σουτζουκια (**Soo-zoo-kee-ah**): Every region produces its own *soo-zoo-Kee-ah*, cured pork sausages seasoned with local spices which vary from region to region.

Σουτζουκια νωπα (**Soo-zoo-kee-ah noh-pah**): These are fresh pork sausages of a pinkish color. They are spiced with fennel seeds and garlic.

Cheese production in Greece is excellent, in terms of quantity as well as quality, though limited to only a few types. The only Greek cheese commonly known outside the country is probably φετα *(feh-tah)*.

In Greece it is customary for cheese to be served as an accompaniment to hors-d'oeuvres or the famous Greek salad, and never at the end of a meal. Whether in a shop or at a restaurant, you can always ask for a taste before deciding on what to buy or order.

Below you will find a brief description of each type, its taste, color, and provenance.

Ανθοτυρο **(Ahn-thoh-tee-roh):** A soft white cheese, salted or unsalted, made from cow's milk. It is mainly produced in Epiros, Crete, and Thrace.

Κασερι **(Kas-ser-ee):** Made from cow's milk, this is quite a strong tasting cheese with a compact golden texture. It is generally used on toasted or grilled slices of bread.

Κεφαλογρουβιερα **(Keh-fah-loh-groo-vee-eh-rah):** With holes similar to Swiss cheese, this type is made from cow's milk or a mixture of cow's and sheep's milk. It is excellent as a garnishing for pasta dishes or soups, and also as an hors-d'oeuvre.

Κεφαλοτυρι **(Keh-fah-loh-tee-ree):** A seasoned, strong cheese made from sheep's milk, it is used solely as a garnishing for pasta.

Μανουρι **(Mah-noo-ree):** A fresh, unsalted cheese made from sheep's milk, this cheese is produced all over Greece. It is very light and digestible.

Μυτζηθρα **(Mee-dzee-thrah):** This is quite a salty goat's or sheep's cheese with a yellow interior. When fresh, it resembles cottage cheese somewhat, and when seasoned, it can be grated over pasta. It is also served as an hors-d'oeuvre.

Φετα **(Feh-tah):** Cow's milk or sheep's milk may be used to make this fresh, white, salty cheese with a firm consistency, preserved in a mixture of milk and salt. It is produced throughout the country.

Χαλουμι **(Hah-loo-mee):** This is a sheep's milk cheese with a soft white interior. It is produced in Cyprus.

Αυγολεμονο **(Av-goh-leh-moh-noh):** A very delicate, creamy sauce made with egg and lemon. It is mainly used to season soups and meat.

Μελιτζανοσαλατα **(Meh-lee-zah-noh-sah-lah-tah):** This sauce consists of roasted eggplant, peeled and blended with oil, onion, salt, and vinegar.

Μπεσαμελλα αλλα ελληνικα **(Beh-shah-mel-lah al-lah el-ee-nee-kah):** A basic beschamel sauce enriched with egg and *keh-fah-loh-tee-ree* cheese.

Σαλτσα λαδολεμονο για λαχανο **(Sal-tsah lah-doh-leh-moh-noh yah lah-hah-noh):** This sauce is made with oil, vinegar or lemon, minced garlic, and mustard. A paste made from black olives may also be added.

Σαλτσα λαδολεμονο για ψαρια **(Sal-tsah lah-doh-leh-moh-noh yah psah-ree-ah):** This sauce is prepared with oil, lemon, salt, pepper, and oregano. It is used to season grilled or barbecued fish.

Σαλτσα με κυμα **(Sal-tsah meh kee-mah):** A tomato and minced meat sauce served with meatpies or spaghetti.

Σαλτσα ντοματες **(Sal-tsah doh-mah-tes):** Oil, onion, parsley, cloves, cumin, and cinnamon are used to prepare this tomato sauce. It is served with pasta or used in stews.

Σαλτσα Σαβορυ **(Sal-tsah sah-voh-ree):** This sauce is prepared with garlic and rosemary fried in oil with a pinch of flour, and vinegar or red wine. It is used to season freshly fried fish.

Σκορδαλια **(Skor-dah-lee-ah):** A sauce prepared with crushed garlic blended with soaked pieces of bread, oil, lemon, and vinegar. The bread may sometimes be replaced by mashed potatoes.

Ταραμοσαλατα **(Tah-rah-moh-sah-lah-tah):** Fish eggs blended with olive oil, lemon, just a touch of onion, potatoes(boiled and then seasoned with dill) are then spread over slices of bread and served as an appetizer.

Τζατζικι **(Zah-zee-kee):** Fresh minced cucumber, garlic, mint or dill, and olive oil are added to a base of Greek yoghurt and used to accompany fried vegetables, fish and meat, or alone, on bread, as an appetizer.

The preparing of sweets and pastries in Greece is an ancient art. Like all the peoples of Europe, the Greeks made sweets long before sugar cane was imported from America. To sweeten pastries and blend ingredients, nectar produced by bees or honey was used. The flavors extracted from almond, pistachio, and roasted with honey sesame were familiar to the Greeks even in classical times. Their syrups made with lemon, orange, and tangerine flowers were also famous: warm water and honey, instead of sugar, were used to macerate citrus fruits. Besides these fruits, rose petals and unripe pistachios are main ingredients in sweets recipes in Greece even today. The island of Chios indisputably holds first place in the art of confectionery.

Among the various national specialties, του κουταλιου (*too koo-tah-lee-oo*) are worth special mention. The literal translation of this term is "spoon sweets" and refers to unripe fruit, chopped into small pieces and cooked in syrup. Other popular sweets are του ταψιου (*too tap-see-oo*), which consist of pastry and a filling of dried fruit, butter, and spices, baked, and then while still hot, dowsed with syrup.

Here we suggest other delicious sweets and pastries that are the most popular in Greece.

Αμυγδαλωτα **(Ah-mig-dah-loh-tah):** Cookies made of almond paste filled with chocolate or jam.

Αμυγδαλωτα Υδραϊκα **(Ah-mig-dah-loh-tah ee-dreh-ee-kah):** Cookies typical of the island of Hydra, made with almond paste softened in orange water, then covered in icing sugar.

Γαλακτομπουρεκο **(Gah-lak-toh-boo-reh-koh):** Prepared with the same pastry as *bak-lah-vas*, though its filling is made with milk, semolina, butter, vanilla, and sugar.

SWEETS

As soon as the sweet is taken out of the oven, it is covered with hot syrup and flavored with lemon.

Καϊμάκι (**Ka-ee-<u>mah</u>-kee**): Ice cream and a special cream flavored with *mah-<u>stee</u>-hah*, a drop of aromatic natural syrup extracted from a tree that grows only on the island of Chios.

Καταΐφι (**Kah-tah-<u>ee</u>-fee**): This is the third of the "trio" of traditional baked sweets. Its puff pastry, however, differs from the one used to make *bak-lah-<u>vas</u>*. Called *<u>fee</u>-loh per kah-tah-<u>ee</u>-fee*, a fresh pastry is used, then filled with a mixture of butter, walnuts or pistachios, and flavoring. Once taken out of the oven, the *kah-tah-<u>ee</u>-fee* are dipped in hot syrup made from sugar and spiced with cinnamon.

Κουραμπιεδες (**Koo-rah-bee-<u>eh</u>-des**): Cookies made of butter, flour, almonds and covered in powdered sugar. They have a crumbly texture and are rolled into balls. Usually made at Christmas time.

Λουκουμια (**Loo-<u>koo</u>-mee-ah**): A gelatinous sweet made with vanilla or mastica (aromatic resin) and almonds covered in powdered sugar. The most famous are produced on the island of Siros.

Μελι (**<u>Meh</u>-lee**): Honey. There are many different kinds available, all of excellent quality. Honey with oregano is a must to try, as it is made exclusively in Greece.

Μελομακαρονα (**Meh-loh-mah-<u>kah</u>-roh-nah**): Cookies made with flour, sugar, oil, walnuts, and flavoring. Baked, and just before completely cooked, dipped in honey syrup, they are then baked again for a few minutes. These cookies are often prepared at Christmas time.

Μουσταλευρια **(Moos-tah-lev-ree-ah):** A pudding made from must, cooked with flour, walnuts, sesame, and cinnamon.

Μπακλαβας **(Bak-lah-vahs):** Traditional diamond-shaped sweet. This consists of puff pastry (*fil-loh per bak-lah-vahs*) filled with walnuts, almonds or pistachios, then covered with a hot syrup made from sugar, spiced with cinnamon and cloves.

Παστελια **(Pahs-teh-lee-ah):** A very simple and delicious sweet, prepared with sesame seeds and honey. Found in all regions of Greece. Sometimes instead of sesame, almonds or pistachios may be used.

Παστες **(Pahs-tes):** Various types of cakes, often rectangular, made with custard cream, chocolate, cocoa, and whipped cream.

Ριζογαλο **(Ree-soh-gah-loh):** Pudding made with rice cooked in sweetened milk and flavored with lemon rind and cinnamon.

Σκαλτσουνια **(Skal-tsoo-nee-ah):** A rather hard cakelike sweet made with all types of dried fruit, including walnuts and raisins.

Σοκολατακια **(Soh-koh-lah-tah-kee-ah):** This refers to chocolates of all kinds, from the simplest milk chocolates to those filled with fruit, liqueur, or cream. Similar to Swiss chocolates.

Χαλβας **(Hal-vahs):** A sweet made with sesame seed butter, almonds or pistachios, chocolate, and sugar. Sold by the kilo.

Χαλβας με σιμιγδαλι **(Hal-vahs meh see-meeg-dah-lee):** A semolina and walnut pudding, browned with butter and then covered in syrup.

WINES

Ancient Greece's love for wine was a veritable cult. Vine cultivation was considered a sign of civilization: literature, religion, and art were permeated with this worship and wherever Greek colonies settled, the planting of vineyards was the first concern.

The custom of drinking fermented drinks goes back to the dawn of time and is common to all peoples, but the ancient Greeks may definitely be considered the fathers of viticulture. They were the first to introduce the technique of pruning and to discover that paradoxically, the poorest soil, the least favorable for other crops, yielded in fact the best wines. Today, about half of all Greek wine is resin-treated. The famous *ret-see-nah* is a white or red wine aged with the adding of some resin (*mahs-tee-kah*). The adding of resin helps in the preservation of wine in high temperatures, but also gives it a bitter taste, which is difficult to appreciate for those who aren't used to it.

There are, however, many wines that do not contain resin – perhaps ones that we find more pleasant – produced particularly in the Peloponnese (in Acacia and Messenia), in Arcadia and on the islands of Cephalonia, Santorini, Samos, Corfu and Zante.

Below you will find a basic list of wines in alphabetical order which represent the most popular varieties. Their origin or the area of production is also specified.

Αρκαδια (**Ar-kah-dee-ah**): Produced in the Peloponnese. This is a dry white wine. It is served with seafood and fish in general.

Αττικη (**At-tee-kee**): This wine is named after its region, Attica. It is a white wine without resin, ideal with fish dishes.

Αχαϊα (**Ah-hah-ee-ah**): Produced in the Peloponnese. It is a sweet red wine. Excellent with desserts and dried fruit.

Δεμεστηχα **(De-mes-tee-hah):** White wine, produced in the Sterea Ellada region. It is also available flavored with resin. Served with appetizers or fish.

Εκαλη **(Eh-kah-lee):** Produced in Attica, this is one of Greece's dry white wines. Very good with seafood and fish dishes.

Καβα Καμπα **(Kah-vah kam-bah):** The region of production is the Peloponnese. A dry red wine, it is mainly served with game.

Κισσαμος **(Kis-sah-mos):** Produced in Crete, this is a sweet red wine served with main-course meat dishes.

Κνωσσος **(Knos-sos):** A red wine produced in Crete. Its heavy syrupy taste makes it particularly good to accompany dried or fresh fruit.

Κουρος **(Koo-ros):** Wine produced in Thessaly. White, sparkling, it is served with fish dishes or appetizers.

Κουρτακι **(Koor-tah-kee):** Produced in Attica, this dry white wine is flavored with r*et-see-nah*. It is usually served at the beginning of a meal with *tah meh-tseh-dah-kee-ah* (appetizers).

Μαντινια **(Mahn-tee-nee-ah):** This dry red wine is produced by the vineyards of Crete. Excellent with red meats.

Μαυροδαφνη **(Mav-roh-dah-fnee):** Produced in the region of Sterea Ellada, red and sweet, it is a very fine dessert wine.

Μοσχατο **(Mohs-hah-toh):** Produced in Attica, this is a sweet red wine. Recommended with fruit.

Μυστρα **(Mees-trah):** A white wine from the Peloponnese, dry tasting.

Νεστωρ **(Nes-tor):** From the Samos vineyards. A sweet red wine.

Παλινη **(Pahl-lee-nee):** A red wine recommended with red meat dishes, produced by the wine-makers of Lesbos.

Πινδος **(Pin-dos):** This is a dry white wine produced in Epirus. Good with seafood or fish in general.

Ροδιτις **(Roh-dee-tis):** Produced in Rhodes. A white wine with a fruity taste. Served with sweets and pastries.

Τσανταλη **(Tsan-dah-lee):** From the vines of Thessaly, both white and rosé varieties are produced. With its delicate taste, it may be served with openers as well as main courses.

Υμητος **(Ee-mee-tos):** The region of its production is Attica. A dry rosé, it is generally served with hors-d'oeuvres.

Φιλερι **(Fee-leh-ree):** The vines which produce this wine grow in Crete. It is a dry tasting red wine. Excellent with red meats.

In a country that boasts such a rich wine production, we should expect to find an equally exciting variety of liqueurs. And indeed, throughout Greece, all over the peninsula as well as on the islands such as Samos, Chios, Crete, Rhodes, a vast range of alcoholic beverages are produced which are often obtained from the macerating of balsamic or aromatic herbs in alcohol. The island of Chios deserves special mention: the famous confectionery and liqueur industries have made their mark in the world of Greek gastronomy. To list all the brands with their characteristics and producers would require a great many pages. We will therefore have to mention only the best known and most popular ones among them.

Καρυδι **(Kah-<u>ree</u>-dee):** A walnut liqueur found in all parts of Greece.

Κουμ Κουατ **(Koom koo-aht):** A sweet-tasting orange or green-colored liqueur, made from Japanese oranges that are also grown on the island of Corfu. A Corfu specialty.

Λεμονι **(Leh-<u>moh</u>-nee):** Strong, though with a very fine lemon taste. It is served on the rocks.

Μαστιχα **(Mahs-<u>tee</u>-hah):** A very fragrant, fruity liqueur produced on the island of Chios. It is often served as an after dinner drink.

Μεταξα **(Meh-tah-<u>ksah</u>):** This is the most famous brandy in all of Greece, very fragrant and distinctive. Produced in the Peloponnese, it appears on the market in three categories (seven, five, or three stars), depending on its age.

Μυστρα Ουζο **(Mis-<u>trah</u> oo-zoh):** A white liqueur with a dry taste, flavored with aniseed. It is diluted with water or ice and served as an aperitif.

Ολυμπος **(Oh-lim-bos):** As its name suggests, this is considered the "liqueur of the gods," probably due to its strong taste. It is usually served as an after dinner drink.

Ρακι **(Rah-kee):** A very pungent aromatic liqueur that resembles the Italian *grappa*.

Here is a list (necessarily a summary) of delicious Greek specialties not included in the categories already covered (cheeses, cold cuts, sweets, etc.), but which nevertheless it would be a shame to miss if you are visiting the country. Also included are those called for in the recipes of various typical dishes.

Αμυγδαλο (**ah-mig-dah-loh**): This drink, made from almonds, is produced in all the Aegean islands where almonds are widely grown. It is well known by the name σουμαδα (*soo-mah-dah*). Extremely refreshing when mixed with ice water.

Αμπελοφυλλα (**Am-beh-loh-fil-lah**): These are very tender vine leaves, boiled and preserved in brine. They are used to prepare rice rolls, known as *dol-mah-dah-kee-ah* (see "National Dishes").

Ανθογαλα (**Ahn-thoh-gah-lah**): One of the finest kinds of butter, it is especially used in the preparation of sweets.

Ανιθο (**Ah-nee-thoh**): Also known in other countries, though perhaps less widely used, dill is an herb used fresh (never dried) in Greek cuisine to season plain meats. Sold in greengrocers' shops or supermarkets, its taste resembles wild fennel.

Βυσσινο (**Vis-see-noh**): This is a type of sweet made with sour black cherries in syrup. The syrup, diluted with water, is an extremely refreshing drink (Vissinada).

Κουλουρακια (**Koo-loo-rah-kee-ah**): A general term for all Greek biscuits, sweet or savoury. The ones sold by street vendors are larger and called "koulouria" (*koo-loo-ree-ah*). They are made with sesame and are usually eaten as snacks.

OTHER SPECIALTIES

Μαχλεπι (**Mah-leh-pee**): This spice is mainly used in leavened bread, *tsoo-reh-kee*. Mah-*leh*-pee is the heart of a wild cherry stone and has a syrupy sweet and aromatic taste.

Μπαμιες (**Bah-mee-es**): Okra – a type of very delicate quite bland vegetable excellent with stewed meats.

Πιτες για σουβλακια (**Pee-tes yah soov-lah-kee-ah**): Small pieces of plain white pizza crust eaten generally with skewers of meat.

Σπο. ακια (**Spoh-rah-kee-ah**): Salted sunflower seeds, shelled and eaten as a snack at any time of the day.

Ταραμας (**Tah-rah-mahs**): Fish eggs mainly used to prepare appetizers.

Ταχινι (**Tah-hee-nee**): Sesame seed butter used in sweets such as *halvas* or the soup *tah-hee-nee* (see "National Dishes").

Φυλλο για καταϊφι (**Fil-loh yah kah-tah-ee-fee**): Pastry used to make *kah-tah-ee-fee* (see "Sweets and Pastries"). Available in pastry shops.

Φυλλο για μπακλαβα (**Fil-loh yah bak-lah-vah**): Extremely fine pastry used to make *bak-lah-vah* (see "Sweets and Pastries"). Also used for *gah-lak-toh-boo-reh-koh* (see "Sweets and Pastries").

Greek culinary traditions have undergone various changes,
as always happens in all forms of heritage, with the
intermixing of cultures due to population movements within
the country itself, or with foreign nations. These racial
integrations (traumatic and involuntary in the case of
conquest; less brutal in other instances) helped to spread
eating habits nationwide which until then were considered
purely local traditions.

This phenomenon of course applies not only to Greece. All
cultures in the world learned early in history to "import"
good ideas and pleasant customs. Just as, for example,
Southern fried chicken or New England clam chowder in the
United States were once regional specialties that became
national favorites (and you can certainly think of examples in
every country in the world), so, many Greek dishes now
prepared throughout the country were originally dishes
typical of a specific region. In the case of Greece,
terminology underwent slight alterations during the period of
Turkish rule as mentioned in our introduction.

You will find below a list of the most widespread dishes in
Greece, the ones most representative of Greek cuisine. Each
dish is given with its name in Greek, followed by the
pronunciation in our Roman alphabet, a description of the
dish, and when during a meal it would be served. Of course,
dishes are arranged in alphabetical order according to the
Greek alphabet.

Αγκινάρες αυγολεμονο (**Ah-gee-_nah_-res av-goh-_leh_-moh-
noh**): Artichokes simmered in onions sautéed in oil (or butter),
and seasoned with dill. When cooked, the sauce _av-goh-leh-
moh-noh_ made with eggs and lemon is added. Main course.

Αγκιναρες με αρακα (**Ah-ghee-_nah_-res meh ah-rah-_kah_**):
Artichokes and new peas, simmered in onions sautéed in oil

(or butter), and seasoned with dill. Here, as in the preceding dish, when cooked, the sauce *av-goh-leh-moh-noh* made with eggs and lemon may be added. Main course.

Αγκινάρες με αρνάκι (**Ah-ghee-nah-res meh ar-nah-kee**): Artichokes and lamb simmered in onions sautéed in oil (or butter) and seasoned with wild mint, garlic, and pepper. Main course.

Αρακάς με αγκινάρες (**Ah-rah-kas meh ah-gee-nah-res**): News peas and artichokes simmered in spring onions and dill. Potatoes may be added. Rice and Greek yoghurt may accompany this main dish.

Αρακάς με κρέας (**Ah-rah-kas meh kreh-ahs**): Stew meat and new peas simmered in new onions, dill, and tomato sauce. Potatoes may also be added. At times white rice and Greek yoghurt are served on the side. Main course.

Αρνάκι σουβλας (**Ar-nah-kee soov-lahs**): A whole spring lamb or lamb cooked on the spit over an open fire. The meat is seasoned with garlic, peppers, rosemary, and oregano. Traditional dish served at Easter. Main course.

Αρνάκι σπιτισιο (**Ar-nah-kee spee-tees-see-oh**): Lamb in tomato sauce, with onion, garlic, bay leaf and other spices, braised in red wine. It is often served accompanied by cooked greens, rice, pasta or baked potatoes. Main course.

Αρνάκι φουρνου (**Ar-nah-kee foor-noo**): Roast lamb or spring lamb baked in the oven with garlic, pepper, a dash of white wine, or beer, or lemon. Main course, served with baked potatoes.

Αρνι εξοχικο (**Ahr-nee ex-oh-hee-koh**): Lamb country-style. Meat stewed and seasoned with onion, garlic, oregano, mint, and pepper. Main course usually served with an assortment of vegetables.

Αρνι φρικασε (**Ahr-nee free-kahs-seh**): Lamb prepared according to a very famous recipe, renowned in all of Greece. The meat is stewed with onions, carrots, celery, and dill. Before serving, it is covered in the sauce *av-goh-leh-moh-noh*. Main course.

Αστακος στα καρβουνα (**Ahs-tah-kos stah kar-voo-nah**): Whole lobster. After being scalded, it is grilled with oil, lemon, pepper, and oregano. Hors-d'oeuvre.

Ατζεμ πιλαφ (**Aht-sem pee-laf**): A rice dish made with tomato sauce. It may also be prepared with meat broth and stewed meat. Usually served as a main course, unless it is cooked without meat in which case it is considered a side dish.

Γαλοπουλα γεμιστη (**Gah-loh-poo-lah yeh-mis-tee**): Stuffed turkey, baked in the oven. The stuffing is made with minced meat, rice, boiled chestnuts, onions, sultanas, pine nuts or pistachios, a dash of wine, fennel seeds, cloves, and pepper. Traditionally served as the main course at Christmas time.

Γαριδες βραστες (**Gah-ree-des vrahs-tes**): Stewed crayfish. Usually seasoned with oil, oregano, lemon, and pepper or other sauces, if preferred. Hors-d'oeuvre.

Γαριδες με φετα (**Gah-ree-des meh feh-tah**): Crayfish and cheese cooked in a pan with oil and a little tomato. Hors-d'oeuvre.

Γαριδες τηγανητες **(Gah-<u>ree</u>-des tee-gah-nee-<u>tes</u>):** Fried crayfish. Hors-d'oeuvre.

Γιουβετσι **(Yoo-<u>vet</u>-see):** Lamb or beef stewed in tomato, cooked in the oven in an earthenware pot, seasoned with garlic, juniper, and pepper. Just before completely cooked, small noodles are added. The dish is served in the baking dish, it is sprinkled with *keh-fah-loh-<u>tee</u>-ree* cheese. Main course.

Γιουρβαλακια **(Yoor-vah-<u>lah</u>-kee-ah):** Meat balls made with a mixture of minced meat and rice, seasoned with onion, parsley, and pepper. They are cooked in broth together with vegetables such as zucchini, carrots, potatoes, and celery. When ready, the sauce *av-goh-<u>leh</u>-moh-noh* is then added. Main course.

Θαλασσινα βραστα **(Thah-lahs-see-<u>nah</u> vrah-<u>stah</u>):** Seafood boiled and dressed with mayonnaise or with oil, lemon, oregano and pepper. Hors-d'oeuvre.

Θαλασσινα τηγανητα **(Thah-lahs-see-<u>nah</u> tee-gah-nee-<u>tah</u>):** Fried seafood seasoned with oil, lemon, oregano, and garlic. May also be served with the sauce *zah-zee-kee*. Hors-d'oeuvre.

Θαλασσινα ωμα **(Thah-lahs-see-<u>nah</u> oh-<u>mah</u>):** Raw seafood served with lemon. Hors-d'oeuvre.

Κακαβια **(Kah-kah-vee-<u>ah</u>):** Fish soup. An assortment of various kinds of fish cooked in a soup with onion, garlic, and celery. May be clear, (with the sauce *av-goh-<u>leh</u>-moh-noh* added) or with tomato, and then served with fried slices of bread. Main course.

Καλαμαρακια γεμιστα (**Kah-lah-mah-<u>rah</u>-kee-ah yeh-mis-<u>tah</u>**): Baby squid stuffed with rice, garlic, parsley, pine nuts, Corinth raisins, tomato sauce and a dowsing of white wine. Main course.

Καλαμαρακια κρασατα (**Kah-lah-mah-<u>rah</u>-kee-ah krahs-<u>sah</u>-tah**): Baby squid cooked in a pan with a little white wine, tomato sauce, onion, and spices. May be served with mashed potatoes or white rice. Main course.

Καλαμαρακια τηγανητα με τζατζικι (**Kah-lah-mah-<u>rah</u>-kee-ah tee-gah-nee-<u>tah</u> meh zah-<u>zee</u>-kee**): Baby squid fried with the sauce *zah-<u>zee</u>-kee*. Served as an appetizer.

Κεφτεδες (**Kef-<u>teh</u>-des**): Meat balls made with minced meat and breadcrumbs seasoned with aromatic herbs, mint, onion, and oregano, they are then fried. Hors-d'oeuvre or main course.

Κοκορετσι (**Koh-koh-<u>ret</u>-see**): Lungs and heart of lamb in a sausage case of lamb gut, seasoned with oregano, garlic, and pepper. Barbecued on a spit. This specialty is sold only in rotisseries, in the evening. The price always refers to the cost per kilo.

Κοτολετες αρνι με σαλτσα (**Koh-toh-<u>leh</u>-tes ahr-<u>nee</u> meh <u>sal</u>-tsah**): Lamb chops cooked in tomato sauce and seasoned with onion and oregano. Main course.

Κοτοπουλο καπαμα (**Koh-<u>toh</u>-poo-loh kah-pah-<u>mah</u>**): The recipe is the same for the next dish listed with the only difference being that melon is replaced by wine and tomatoes. It may be served with a side dish of potatoes, spinach, or carrots. Main dish.

Κοτοπουλο λεμονατο **(Koh-<u>toh</u>-poo-loh leh-moh-<u>nah</u>-toh):** Chicken seasoned with lemon, butter, and aromatic herbs and roasted in a casserole. Main dish.

Κοτοπουλο με μπαμιες **(Koh-<u>toh</u>-poo-loh meh <u>bah</u>-mee-es):** Chicken stew with _bah-mee-es_ (see "Other Specialties") cooked in tomato sauce seasoned with dill and onion. Main course.

Κοτοπουλο με χυλοπιτες **(Koh-<u>toh</u>-poo-loh me hee-loh-<u>pee</u>-tes):** Chicken pieces cooked in tomato sauce with onion, oregano or parsley. Before it is thoroughly cooked, _hee-loh-pee-tes_, square-shaped pasta is added. _Kee-fah-loh-<u>tee</u>-ree_ or _keh-fah-loh-groo-vee-<u>eh</u>-rah_ cheese can be sprinkled over it.

Κουκια φρεσκα **(Koo-kee-<u>ah</u> fres-kah):** Tender beans still in the pod cooked in a fried mix of onion and dill. Served with a covering of yoghurt. Main course.

Κρεας κοκκινιστο **(<u>Kreh</u>-ahs koh-kee-nis-<u>toh</u>):** Meat stewed in tomato sauce and spiced with onion, clove and cinnamon. Served with mashed potato or rice. Main course.

Κυδωνια με κρεας **(Kee-<u>doh</u>-nee-ah meh <u>kreh</u>-ahs):** Meat served with quince and flavored with clove and butter. Main course.

Λαγος στιφαδο **(Lah-<u>gos</u> stee-<u>fah</u>-doh):** Stewed hare with spring onion and flavored with juniper, cinnamon, bay, clove, tomato juice and a dowsing of red wine. Main course.

Λακερδα **(Lah-<u>ker</u>-dah):** Large sized fish like swordfish or tuna can be served with this recipe. It is eaten raw, sliced and salted, and with an olive oil dressing. Hors-d'oeuvre.

Μακαροναδα (**Mah-kah-roh-<u>nah</u>-dah**): Pasta (normally spaghetti), seasoned with melted butter, tomato sauce (prepared earlier) and *keh-fah-loh-<u>tee</u>-ree* cheese. Main course or side dish.

Μακαρονια με κρεας (**Mak-kah-<u>roh</u>-nee-ah meh <u>kreh</u>-ahs**): Pasta served with melted butter, the stew's sauce and the same meat. This dish is served with a sprinkling of *keh-fah-loh-<u>tee</u>-ree* or *keh-fah-loh-groo-vee-<u>eh</u>-rah* cheese. Main course.

Μακαρονια με κυμα (**Mah-kah-<u>roh</u>-nee-ah meh kee-<u>mah</u>**): Pasta served with melted butter and ragout. Main course.

Μακαρονια παστιτσιο (**Mah-kah-<u>roh</u>-nee-ah pah-<u>stit</u>-see-oh**): Boiled macaroni, seasoned with ragout and bechamel, a thick white sauce (see "Sauces and Condiments") baked in the oven.

Μαριδες τηγανητες (**Mah-<u>ree</u>-des tee-gah-nee-<u>tes</u>**): Small-sized fish (smelt) floured and fried in olive oil. Served with *zah-<u>zee</u>-kee* sauce. Hors-d'oeuvre.

Μελιτζανες γεμιστες (**Meh-lit-<u>zah</u>-nes yeh-mis-<u>tes</u>**): Eggplants stuffed with rice, onion, tomato, parsley, mint and oil. Baked. Main course.

Μελιτζανες παπουτσακια (**Meh-lit-<u>zah</u>-nes pah-poot-<u>sah</u>-kyah**): Eggplants filled with minced meat, dampened bread, onion, mint, parsley, a smidgen of fresh tomatoes. Baked. Main course.

Μελιτζανες τηγανητες (**Meh-lit-<u>zah</u>-nes tee-gah-nee-<u>tes</u>**): Fried eggplants. Sometimes, before frying, they can be dipped in a batter made of water, flour and barm. These are served with *zah-<u>zee</u>-kee* sauce. Hors-d'oeuvre.

NATIONAL DISHES

Μοσχαρι κρασατο **(Mos-kah-ree kras-sah-toh):** Beef braised in tomato sauce with a dash of red wine together with spices: coriander seed, clove, bay, cumin, oil and onion. Main course.

Μουσακα ζαρζαβατικα **(Moos-sah-kah zar-tsah-vah-tee-kah):** Fried mixed vegetables covered with ragout and bechamel and baked in the oven (see "Sauces and Condiments"). Main course.

Μουσακα μελιτζανες **(Moos-sah-kah meh-lit-zah-nes):** A timbale of fried eggplants covered with ragout sauce and bechamel (see "Sauces and Condiments") Main course.

Μπακαλιαρακια τηγανητα **(Bah-kah-lee-ah-rah-kyah tee-gah-nee-tah):** A fillet of stockfish dipped in a batter of flour, water and barm before frying. The *skor-dah-lee-ah* sauce is added. Hors-d'oeuvre.

Μπακαλιαρος γιαχνι **(Bah-kah-lee-ah-ros yah-nee):** A codfish stew with tomato and boiled chickpeas. Main course.

Μπαμιες γιαχνι **(Bah-mee-es yah-nee):** *Bah-mee-es* or okra (see "Other Specialties") stewed with meat in tomato sauce and flavored with dill and oil. Main course or side dish.

Μπαμιες με κρεας **(Bah-mee-es meh kreh-ahs):** *Bah-mee-es* vegetables (see "Other Specialties") stewed with meat in sauce. Main course.

Μπιφτεκια σκαρας **(Bif-teh-kyah skah-rahs):** Grilled croquettes of minced meat, similar to hamburgers. Main course, served with a variety of side dishes.

Μπουρεκακια **(Boo-reh-kah-kee-ah):** Rolls of pastry stuffed with cheese or minced meat flavored with onion and oregano. They can be baked (*boo-reh-kah-kyah foor-noo*) or fried (*boo-reh-kah-kee-ah tee-gah-nee-tah*). Hors-d'oeuvre.

Ντολμαδακια **(Dol-mah-dah-kyah):** Vine-leaf rolls stuffed with rice, dill, onion, lemon juice and oil. A cold hors-d'oeuvre to be served with yoghurt.

Ντολμαδακια με κυμα **(Dol-mah-dah-kyah meh kee-mah):** Vine-leaf rolls stuffed with meat, dill, onion, lemon juice and oil. Main course to be served with an *av-goh-le-moh-noh* sauce.

Ντολμαδες **(Dol-mah-des):** Boiled cabbage-leaf rolls stuffed with minced meat, rice, onion and parsley. Can be cooked either with tomato or boiled. Main course.

Ντοματες γεμιστες **(Doh-mah-tes yeh-mis-tes):** Tomatoes stuffed with rice, flavored with onion, mint, parsley, pine nuts, sultana grapes, oil and juice of the tomatoes themselves. Baked. Main course.

Ντοματες με αυγα **(Doh-mah-tes meh av-gah):** Eggs cooked in small frying pan with butter and fresh tomato. Main course.

Ντοματοσαλατα **(Doh-mah-toh-sah-lah-tah):** Fresh tomato salad. Side dish.

Ξιφιας σκαρας **(Ksee-fee-ahs skah-rahs):** Slice of grilled swordfish. Main course.

Ξιφιας σουβλακι **(Ksee-fee-ahs soov-lah-kee):** Skewered swordfish cooked over live embers and seasoned with oil, lemon, oregano and pepper. Main course.

NATIONAL DISHES

Οκταποδι κρασατο **(Ok-tah-<u>poh</u>-dee krass-<u>ah</u>-toh):** Braised boiled octopus, dowsed with red wine and flavored with onion, pepper and oregano. Main course, sometimes accompanied by various side dishes.

Οκταποδι με ρυζι **(Ok-tah-<u>poh</u>-dee meh <u>ree</u>-zee):** Stewed octopus with rice, tomato, garlic, pepper and other spices. Main course.

Παπια με μπαμιες **(<u>Pah</u>-pyah meh <u>bah</u>-mee-es):** Duck and okra (see "Other Specialties") stewed with onion, tomato and oil. Main course.

Παπια ψητη **(<u>Pah</u>-pyah psee-<u>tee</u>):** Roast duck cooked in a pot or in the oven, seasoned with butter, lemon and pepper. Main course.

Παπουτσακια **(Pah-poot-<u>sah</u>-kyah):** Eggplants filled with minced meat and rice, flavored with onion, mint, tomato juice and oil. Baked. Main course.

Πατατες μουσακα **(Pah-<u>tah</u>-tes moos-sah-<u>kah</u>):** A pastry shell with potatoes, ragout and bechamel (see "Sauces and Condiments"). Main course.

Πατατες τηγανητες **(Pah-<u>tah</u>-tes tee-gah-nee-<u>tes</u>):** French fries.

Πατατοκεφτεδες **(Pah-tah-toh-kef-<u>teh</u>-des):** Mashed potato croquettes kneaded with milk, butter, eggs, pepper and *kahs-seh-ree* cheese. They are covered with flour before frying. Hors-d'oeuvre.

Πατσας **(Paht-<u>sahs</u>):** Pork tripe cooked in a soup flavored with mint, onion and lemon. It is served chilled. Main course.

Περδικες κρασατες (**Per-dee-kess krahs-sah-tess**): Braised partridge dowsed with wine and flavored with bay, onion, oregano and other spices. Main course.

Πιπεριες γεμιστες (**Pee-peh-ree-es yeh-mis-tes**): Baked bell peppers with rice. The stuffing is made of the same ingredients as tomatoes stuffed with rice. Main course.

Πιπεριες τηγανητες (**Pee-peh-ree-es tee-gah-nee-tes**): Fried bell peppers seasoned with vinegar, parsley and garlic. Hors-d'oeuvre.

Πιπεριες ψητες (**Pee-peh-ree-es psee-tes**); Grilled bell peppers seasoned with oil and vinegar. Hors-d'oeuvre.

Πιτσουνια ψητα/φουρνου (**Pit-soo-nyah psee-tah/foor-noo**): Game marinated for 24 hours in red wine, flavored with various spices and cooked in the oven or wrapped and steamed. Main course.

Ραπανακια σαλατα (**Rah-pah-nah-kyah sah-lah-tah**): Radish salad. Appetizer.

Σαλιγκαρια στιφαδο (**Sah-lee-gah-ree-ah stee-fah-doh**): Snails with stewed boiled onions or with tomato and flavored with spices. Main course.

Σαρδελες λαδοριγανη (**Sar-deh-les lah-doh-ree-gah-nee**): Sardines seasoned with oil and oregano. Baked. Main course.

Σελινοριζες με χοιρινο (**Seh-lee-noh-ree-zehs meh hee-ree-noh**): Stewed or roasted pork with chopped celery roots. After cooking, add the *av-goh-leh-moh-noh* sauce. Main course.

Σουβλακια (**Soov-<u>lah</u>-kyah**): Flavored meat on skewers with oregano, pepper, lemon and parsely. Main course. A variation is with the skewers wrapped in Greek (*pee-tah*) pizza with fresh tomato, onion and *zah-<u>zee</u>-kee* sauce. In such a case, a simple snack.

Σουπιες με σαλτσα (**Soo-pee-<u>es</u> me <u>sahl</u>-tsah**): Stewed cuttlefish with tomato sauce. Main course accompanied with various side dishes.

Σουπιες τηγανητες (**Soo-pee-<u>es</u> tee-gah-nee-<u>tes</u>**): Cuttlefish flavored and fried consumed as an hors-d'oeuvre.

Σπανακοπιτα (**Spah-nah-<u>koh</u>-pee-tah**): Pastry stuffed with *feh*-tah cheese and spinach, baked. It is similar to the Continental country pies. Hors-d'oeuvre.

Σπανακορυζο (**Spah-nah-<u>koh</u>-ree-zoh**): Risotto (an Italian dish of rice) with spinach, flavored with onion and dill. It is served with *av-goh-<u>leh</u>-moh-noh* sauce. Main course.

Συκωτακια τηγανητα (**See-koh-<u>tah</u>-kyah tee-gah-nee-<u>tah</u>**): Fried slices of pig's liver seasoned with lemon. Hors-d'oeuvre.

Συκωτακια ψητα σκαρας (**See-koh-<u>tah</u>-kyah psee-<u>tah</u> skah-rahs**): Grilled slices of pig's liver flavored with oil, oregano, mustard and pepper. Hors-d'oeuvre.

Ταχινοσουπα (**Tah-hee-<u>noh</u>-soo-pah**): Crushed sesame seed soup. Main course.

Τραχανας (**Trah-hah-<u>nahs</u>**): Home-made soup alphabet with flour, eggs, yoghurt or curdled milk, a smidgen of tomato.

When the soup alphabet dries, it is cooked in a broth. Main course.

Τσιρος (**Tsee-ross**): Smoked anchovies, seasoned with oil, dill and lemon. Consumed as an hors-d'oeuvre.

Φαβα σουπα (**Fah-vah soo-pah**): Cream of dried broad beans or dried peas boiled and seasoned with oil and lemon. Main course.

Φακες (**Fah-kess**): Lentil soup seasoned with garlic, dried bay leaves, with olive oil a little wine vinegar added before serving. Main course.

Φασολαδα (**Fahs-soh-lah-dah**): Bean soup cooked with tomato, onion, carrot, celery and olive oil. Main course.

Φρικασε (**Free-kahs-seh**): Lamb or kid meat, cooked with lettuce and flavored with green onions and dill. It is served with *av-goh-leh-moh-noh* sauce. Main course.

Ψαρια φρεσκα (**Psah-ree-ah fress-kah**): Fresh fish wrapped and steamed, grilled or baked. Flavored with garlic, oil and lemon. Main course.

Ψαρι παλαμιδα (**Psah-ree pah-lah-mee-dah**): A variety of typical fish of the Aegean Sea, not common elsewhere. Similar to tuna fish and consumed in slices, usually cooked wrapped and steamed, or grilled and seasoned with a sauce of oil, lemon and oregano. Main course.

REGIONAL DISHES

Although it would be interesting and intriguing to mention all the characteristic regional delicacies, the list would become much too long and dispersive. Therefore, we shall limit ourselves to describing the "regional versions" of the better known national dishes. An exception will be made, however, for some extremely popular local dishes. As for the most famous typical dishes, we shall provide the name, the ingredients and their rating on the menu. The list is subdivided into regions.

THRACE

This region produces delicious cheeses, exquisite yoghurt, aromatic cold meats containing aniseed, dried fish (but there is certainly no lack of fresh fish). Sweets with fresh butter are renowned, too. There are also vegetables and a great quantity of greens and (fresh or dried) seasonal fruit. Many culinary specialties of this region find their way to the tables of the entire nation and often are also known abroad.

Μπομποτα με μπριζολες χοιρινες **(Bom-boh-tah meh bree-zoh-les hee-ree-nes):** Maize pudding cooked in Greek fashion, with pork chops in tomato sauce. Main course.

Παστουρμας: **(Pahs-toor-mahs):** This is a type of raw ham of camel meat or beef, flavored with garlic and strong cayenne pepper. It is eaten sliced, raw or fried. Hors-d'oeuvre.

Σαλαμια διαφορα **(Sah-lah-mee-ah dee-ah-foh-rah):** Various cold cuts made with pork or wild boar, flavored with aniseed and red pepper. Served as an hors-d'oeuvre.

Σουτζουκια (**Soo-zoo-kee-ah**): seasoned piccant sausages of pork with grains of pepper. They are fried with eggs in a pan but can also be served cooked with other recipes, as an hors-d'oeuvre.

Τυροπιτα Θρακικη (**Tee-roh-pee-tah thrah-kee-kee**): A *feh-tah* cheese pizza. This is a homemade pastry baked flat, covered with butter. Main course.

Χαλβας Θρακιωτικος (**Hal-vahs trah-kee-oh-tee-kos**): A sweet made with hard grain semolina, with sugar syrup and butter. Flavors like vanilla or lemon can be used to lighten the taste of the nuts added toward the end of the cooking. Served hot and covered with cinnamon.

MACEDONIA

The extensive region is rich in agriculture: rice, maize, corn and rye (the largest production in the entire Hellenic territory). This is the reason why it boasts of an enormous quantity of typical products. The production of milk and dairy produce is excellent and very popular.
Among the typical foodstuffs of Macedonia or rather of northern Greece, are the κασερι *(kahs-seh-ree)* cheese, the ταχινι *(tah-hee-nee)*, a kind of butter derived from sesame seeds, and the wines. According to culinary experts, this kind of cooking is one of the most tasteful cuisines of all the Greek regions.

Αγριοπαπια σαλμι (**Ah-gree-oh-pah-pee-ah sahl-mee**): Wild duck cooked in salmi. Like all salmi dishes, it is cooked after having been marinated with red wine and

flavored with bay, small onions, cumin seeds and dill.
Main course.

Κασερι πεϊνιρλι (**Kahs-<u>seh</u>-ree pehee-neer-<u>lee</u>**): A baked or
fried folded pizza pie stuffed with *kahs-<u>seh</u>-ree* cheese.
Hors-d'oeuvre.

Λαδερα γιαχνι (**Lah-deh-<u>rah</u> yah-nee**): *<u>Bah</u>-mee-ess* (okra:
see "Other Specialties", marrows or eggplants stewed in oil,
onion and tomato sauce.

Μπακαλιαρος σκορδαλια (**Bah-kah-lee-<u>ah</u>-ross skor-dah-
lee-<u>ah</u>**): Fillets of dried codfish coated in a batter of flour,
water and barm and cooked in olive oil. Served hot with
cold garlic sauce. Hors-d'oeuvre.

Μπουγατσα Θεσσαλονικης (**Boo-<u>gaht</u>-tsah thess-ah-loh-<u>nee</u>-
kis**): Rolls of puff pastry filled with *<u>feh</u>-tah* cheese, baked.
Eaten hot, covered with a coating of sugar. A snack.

Παπια με μπαμιες (**<u>Pah</u>-pee-ah meh <u>bah</u>-mee-es**): Duck and
<u>bah</u>-mee-es (okra: see "Other Specialties") stewed in tomato
sauce seasoned with onion and dill. Main course.

Πατσας (**Paht-<u>sas</u>**): Boiled pork with rice covered with pork
tripe jelly and seasoned with mint or dill. Main course.

Ποικιλια ψαρια ψητα (**Pee-kee-<u>lee</u>-ah <u>psah</u>-ree-ah psee-
<u>tah</u>**): A mixture of grilled or ember-cooked fish served with
lemon sauce, oregano, oil, mustard, garlic and minced
cabbage. Main course.

Σπανακορυζο (**Spah-nah-<u>koh</u>-ree-zoh**): Boiled rice with
spinach, flavored with onion and dill. After it is cooked,

av-goh-leh-moh-noh sauce is added. The result is a cream over which small pieces of *feh-tah* cheese are sprinkled. Main course.

Ταχινοσουπα **(Tah-hee-noh-soo-pah):** A soup of crushed sesame cooked in a broth. After cooking, it turns into a cream which requires no dressing although fine bread crumbs are usually added. Main course.

Χοιρινο με σελινοριζα **(Hee-ree-noh meh seh-lee-noh-ree-zah):** Pork pieces stewed with celery and flavored with onion and pepper. Main course.

THESSALY

The method of cooking in this region varies according to the province. Yet it may be said that the basic foodstuffs are those "of the land." Corn and other cereals are predominant in the cooking in this region. The fish comes only from the eastern coast and consumption is not very high. In fact, the specialties of this area are all based on meats and wheat but much use is made of other types of national dishes.

Κοκορετσι Καρδιτσας **(Koh-koh-ret-tsee Kar-deet-sahs):** A fry of pork, or chicken, or lamb cooked over live coals. Flavored with oil, lemon, garlic, oregano and pepper. Hors-d'oeuvre.

Κρεας αρνι κοκκινιστο **(Kreh-ahs ahr-nee koh-kee-nis-toh):** Baked lamb in tomato sauce seasoned with onion and spices. It is accompanied by various dressings. Main course.

REGIONAL DISHES

Παστιτσιο Ολυμπου **(Pahs-teet-see-oh Oh-leem-poo):** A timbale of long pasta flavored with bechamel (see "Sauces and Condiments") and ragout.

Ριγανοκεφτεδες **(Ree-gah-noh-kef-teh-des):** Fried croquettes of boiled mashed potatoes mixed with fisheggs *(tah-rah-mah)* and flavored generously with oregano, lemon juice, oil and onion. Hors-d'oeuvre.

Στρυφτη η κλωστοπιτα Θεσσαλιας **(Strif-tee ee klos-toh-pee-tah Thess-ah-lee-ahs):** Puff pastry filled with *feh-tah* cheese, beaten eggs and spices. Baked. Hors-d'oeuvre.

Χαλβας Φαρσαλων **(Hal-vas Far-sah-lon):** Sweet made with semolina, butter, flavors, a coating of icing sugar and almonds.

EPIRUS

A vast and variegated mountainous region. The geographical position reflects its characteristics also in its cooking methods, where kid's meat and lamb, cheeses, butter and yoghurt prevail. Greens are also evident in large quantities.

Αρνακι κλεφτικο **(Ahr-nah-kee klef-tee-koh):** Spring lamb in small pieces cooked with the entrails and potatoes (or vegetables) in the oven. Main course.

Κουκια με γιαουρτι **(Koo-kee-ah meh yah-oor-tee):** Dried broad beans cooked in an onion sauce with oil and bacon. They may also be cooked with meat. Served with yoghurt. Main course.

Κρεατοπιτα (**Kreh-ah-<u>toh</u>-pee-tah**): Baked pie of minced meat with sauce wrapped in a puff pastry.
Hors-d'oeuvre.

Μπακλαβας Ιωαννινων (**Bak-lah-<u>vas</u> loh-ah-<u>nee</u>-non**): A sweet in a homemade puff pastry, full of dried fruit (nuts or almonds) together with spices and sugar syrup.

Τυροπιτα Ιωαννινων (**Tee-<u>roh</u>-pee-tah loh-ah-<u>nee</u>-non**): Homemade puff pastry with _feh_-tah cheese, eggs and spices.
Hors-d'oeuvre.

STEREA ELLAS (CENTRAL GREECE)

This cuisine is very much like that of Epirus, differing only in the more frequent presence of fish on the menu thanks to the region's long coastline. Besides shellfish, seafood and fresh fish, lightly and quickly barbecued, or simply boiled, sun-dried or smoked fish are also available.

Αρνακι λεμονατο (**Ahr-<u>nah</u>-kee leh-moh-<u>nah</u>-toh**): Spring lamb flavored with onion and spices (cardamom, clove, etc.) cooked in a pot with lemon juice. It looks like braised beef without wine. Main course. Usually served with vegetables, or rice, or baked potatoes.

Κοτοπιτα (**Koh-<u>toh</u>-pee-tah**): Rustic pizza with a filling of chicken, onion, celery, egg and cheese. Hors-d'oeuvre.

Πιτα με πρασα (**<u>Pee</u>-tah meh <u>prahs</u>-sah**): savourypie made with puff pastry filled with cheese and leeks which have been previously cooked in butter with egg and bechamel (see "Sauces and Condiments"). Hors-d'oeuvre.

Τυροπιτα Ρουμελιωτικη **(Tee-<u>roh</u>-pee-tah Roo-meh-lee-<u>oh</u>-tee-kee):** Baked puff pastry pie of <u>feh</u>-tah cheese with milk, egg, butter and pepper. Hors-d'oeuvre.

Ψαρι πλακι **(Psah-ree plah-kee):** Large-size fish (of sea bream or swordfish type) baked with onion, parsley, sugar, white wine and a bit of tomato. Potatoes and olive oil to add. Main course.

Ψαρια τηγανητα **(Psah-ree-ah tee-gah-nee-<u>tah</u>):** Medium-size fish floured and fried in olive oil. Served with *sah-voh-ree* sauce. Main course.

PELOPONNESE

This region's cuisine is extremely varied in produce. North Peloponnese is predominantly vineyards, orchards (especially citrus fruits) sugar beet and potato. The Corinthian potato is among the tastiest in the entire Mediterranean. This region is also the homeland of the "sultana," the grape of Corinth, white and seedless, very sweet in taste and world famed. The Kalamàta olives are also very famous. Fish is often present since fishing is carried out in all the seas surrounding the peninsula.

Πατατες με αυγα **(Pah-<u>tah</u>-tes meh av-<u>gah</u>):** Omelette with fried potatoes and *keh-fah-loh-<u>tee</u>-ree* or *kahs-<u>seh</u>-ree* cheese. Main course.

Πατατες σε τουρτα **(Pah-<u>tah</u>-tes seh <u>toor</u>-tah):** Mashed potato pie with mixed <u>feh</u>-tah cheese, oregano, bechamel (see "Sauces and Condiments") and eggs. Baked. Main course.

Πηλιον σπετσοφαϊ (**Pee-lee-on spet-soh-fa-ee**): Stewed sausages cooked with eggplants and green chili. Main course.

Φρουταλια (**Froot-ah-lee-ah**): Omelette with sausage and potato, flavored with mint and butter. Main course.

THE ISLANDS

The major islands provide the most famous regional versions of the national dishes. However, the rest of the Greek archipelago also offers a surprising variety of dishes which are too numerous to describe.

CYPRUS

Politically speaking, the island of Cyprus does not belong to Greece, although Greek is also spoken there. This is why we are mentioning it in this chapter. The internal areas are characterized by mountainous ranges with gentle peaks and the climate is always mild. As for the cuisine, fish is an important part of the diet in the coastal areas, while the hinterland offers dishes based mostly on meat, cheeses and vegetables.

Γουρουνοπουλο με κολοκασι (**Goo-roo-noh-poo-loh meh koh-loh-kahs-see**): A whole piglet flavored with garlic, fresh onions, oil, pepper and tomato, baked together with the *koh-loh-kahs-see* vegetables (a root plant similar to the Jerusalem artichoke; the taste resembles that of the sweet potato). Main course.

Καλαμαρακια στο φουρνο (**Kah-lah-mah-<u>rah</u>-kyah-ah stoh <u>foor</u>-no**): Small baked squid stuffed with rice, onion, spices, flavors (parsely, sage) and dowsed with wine. Main course.

Μαριδες τηγανητες (**Mah-<u>ree</u>-des teeh-gah-nee-<u>tes</u>**): Minute fish (eperlani) fried in olive oil and served hot and crunchy with lemon and *zah-<u>zee</u>-kee* sauce.

Μπουρεκια με χαλουμι (**Boo-<u>reh</u>-kyah meh hah-<u>loo</u>-mee**): Fried flat pies full of *hah-<u>loo</u>-mee*, a typically Cypriot cheese. Hors-d'oeuvre.

Οκταποδι κρασατο (**Ok-tah-<u>poh</u>-dee krahs-<u>sah</u>-toh**): Braised polyp flavored with cinnamon, nutmeg and dowsed with red wine. Served with slightly fried peppers. Hors-d'oeuvre.

Πατσας (**Paht-<u>sahs</u>**): Lamb tripe stewed with brain and tongue, flavored with clove, bay, celery, onion and carrot. Main course.

Πομπαρι (**Pom-<u>bah</u>-ree**): Lamb's entrails stuffed with minced meat, rice, onion, tomato and oregano. Cooked in pot with butter and olive oil. Main course.

Σαρκεσαδα (**Sahr-keh-<u>sah</u>-dah**): Vegetable soup (carrot, celery, onion, potato) and meat cubes of lamb or pigeon (one for each serving). When cooked, *av-goh-<u>leh</u>-moh-noh sauce* is added. Main course.

Τσχορβα σουπα (**Tshor-vah <u>soo</u>-pah**): Wheat grain soup, thin spaghetti and fresh plum tomatoes. It is flavored with onion and pepper and accompanied by fried croutons. Main course.

CRETE

It is the "wildest" island of Greece, from a geographical viewpoint. Its primitive nature has influenced the social geography and is also reflected in its cuisine. Often, game plays a leading role on the local cooking list, but also kid meat, partridge or wild boar. Over and above the consumption of meat, the eating habits are also based on homemade pastry, cheeses and fruit. Naturally, fish and mollusks are also served frequently.

Καλτσουνια (**Kahl-<u>tsoo</u>-nee-ah**): Butter-milk curd pies wrapped in salted puff pastry with sesame seeds (both in and over the pastry). Baked. Hors-d'oeuvre.

Κρεατοπιτα Κριτης (**Kreh-ah-<u>toh</u>-pee-tah <u>kree</u>-tis**): Boned leg of kid flavored with oregano or mint and a dash of wine, all wrapped in homemade pastry covered with sesame seeds. Baked. Main course.

Σκαλτσουνια κριτικα (**Skal-<u>tsoo</u>-nee-ah kree-tee-<u>kah</u>**): This is a kind of Sienese cake in Cretan fashion full of nuts and other dried fruit and covered with orange blossom syrup and a coating of sugar.

RHODES

Rhodes is the capital of the Dodecanese and is the largest island of the twelve which form the archipelago. The arid land has rendered the islands the poorest areas anywhere in Greece. Yet their beauty has compensated for the scarcity of cultivation. In fact, over the past thirty years, tourist development has overtaken that of agriculture. The natural attractions and the constant mild climate have turned them into a great tourist resort. The outstanding resource, as far as food is concerned, is fish. The wines, too, are well known. The island's cuisine has succumbed to the influence of foreign traditions, particularly those of nearby Italy, especially after World War II.

Μακαρονια φουρνου (**Mah-kah-roh-nee-ah foor-noo**): Baked macaroni with a sauce of stewed meat. This name also applies to all timbales made with all types of pasta. Main course.

Σπληναντερο στο φουρνο (**Splee-nahn-deh-roh stoh foor-noh**): Lamb's entrails with a dressing of lemon juice, garlic, pepper, oregano, feh-tah or mee-zee-thrah cheese, parsley, and wrapped in a net of intestines. Baked with oil and potatoes. Main course.

Φασολακια με κρεας (**Fahs-soh-lah-kee-ah meh kreh-ahs**): Meat stew cooked with coral beans, flavored with onion, fresh tomato and parsely. Main course.

Ψαρι ροδιτικο (**Psah-ree roh-dee-tee-koh**): Typical fish of Rhodes which is either grilled or placed over live embers, seasoned with garlic, rosemary, lemon and oil. Main course.

SAMOS

Samos is famous for its muscat wines. But it is not only the vines that grow well in this soil. Huge plantations yield fruit in abundance and there is also a good production of vegetables. However, fishing and flock and herd breeding are the main activities of its inhabitants.

Κρεμυδοπιτα **(Kreh-mee-_doh_-pee-tah):** savourypie filled with _feh-tah_ cheese and onion or leek flavored with a dash of muscat wine. Hors-d'oeuvre.

Λαχανοπιτα **(Lah-hah-_noh_-pee-tah):** savoury pie of Savoy cabbage with sausage and a dash of wine. Hors-d'oeuvre.

Σπανακοπιτες **(Spah-nah-_koh_-pee-tes):** Tartlets filled with _mee-_zee_-trah_ cheese and spinach. A snack.

CHIOS

It is famous for its culinary art dating back to ancient times but mostly is known for its industry of confectionery. The island of Chios boasts one characteristic which renders it unique: the mastic tree from which a particular flavored substance is extracted. The mastic (which looks like a kind of "tear-drop" oozing out of the bark), used in cooking to provide a characteristic taste to the food.
Orchards covering large areas of land supply the typical produce of this island, together with a variety of vegetables.
When the greens are still sour, they are used as main ingredients to cook sweets.

Ανθος λεμονιας **(Ahn-_thos_ leh-moh-nee-_ahs_):** Sweetmeats of syruped lemon blossoms.

Γλυκα του κουταλιου **(Glee-_kah_ too koo-tah-lee-_oo_):** Sweetmeats of orange, lemon, or sour black cherry, blossom in thick syrup.

Μαστιχα γλυκο (**Mahs-<u>tee</u>-hah ghlee-<u>koh</u>**): Sugar kneaded with mastic. It becomes a thick, soft glaze of white crystalline paste, and is eaten by dipping a spoonful of this sweet in a glass of cold water.

Μελιτζανακι (**Meh-liz-ah-<u>nah</u>-kee**): A sweet made out of eggplants picked while still tiny and cooked in syrup.

Οσπρια με μυδια (**<u>Ohs</u>-pree-ah meh <u>mee</u>-dee-ah**): Vegetables with stewed mussels, flavored with onion, dill and oil. Main course.

Σουτζουκια Σμυρνεϊκα (**Soo-<u>zoo</u>-kee-ah Smir-<u>neh</u>-ee-kah**): Fried meat balls kneaded with biscuit slices, flavored with garlic and cumin, covered with biscuit crumbs. Served with tomato sauce and a rice side dish. This dish comes from the city of Smirna in Asia Minor. Main course.

Τριανταφυλλο γλυκο (**Tree-ahn-<u>dah</u>-fil-loh glee-<u>koh</u>**): Sweetmeat of rose petals in a thick syrup.

Φυστικι γλυκο του κουταλιου (**Fis-<u>tee</u>-kee glee-<u>koh</u> too koo-tah-lee-<u>oo</u>**): Sweetmeat of bitter green pistachio in a thick syrup.

LESBOS (OR MYTILENE)

This island is very close to Chios. Both climate and geographical layout are very similar to those of Chios and also the produce is identical: fruit, vegetables, greens, olives and fish.

Γιουσλεμεδες **(Yoos-leh-meh-des):** Savoury pastries filled with *mee-zee-thrah* cheese. They are either fried or baked. Hors-d'oeuvre.

Ορτυκια πιλαφ **(Or-tee-kee-ah pee-laf):** Quail browned in fried onion and then cooked in a broth with rice. Main course.

IONIAN ISLANDS

The Ionian islands extend from the island of Corfu to the island of Kîthira. They are also known as the archipelago of the seven islands of the Ionian Sea.
The cuisine is based on fish and molluscs, rice, greens, veal, goat or sheep meat and cheeses.

Γαριδες σαγανακι **(Gah-ree-des sah-gah-nah kee):** Crayfish with sauce, pan-cooked and seasoned with *feh-tah* cheese and butter. Main course. (Zante).

Γοπες τηγανητες με σαβορι **(Goh-pes tee-gah-nee-tes meh sah-voh-ree):** Fried fish with *sah-voh-ree* sauce. Main course. (Lef Katha).

Κρεατοπιτα Κεφαλονιτικη **(Kreh-ah-toh-pee-tah Keh-fah-loh-nee-tee-kee):** A lean lamb pie. The meat is fried in butter with garlic, white wine and parsley, then cooked in a pot with rice and tomato. Rolled in puff pastry with *feh-tah* cheese and hard boiled eggs, it is then baked.
Main course (Cephalonia).

Μπεκατσες κρασατες **(Beh-kaht-ses kras-sah-tes):** Woodcocks braised in red wine with butter, onion, fresh tomato sauce. Main course (Cephalonia).

Μπουρδετο (**Boor-<u>deh</u>-toh**): Boiled sea scorpion dipped in tomato sauce and paprika. Main course (Corfu).

Σοφριτο (**Sof-<u>freet</u>-toh**): Floured slices of veal, fried and seasoned with oil, salt, pepper and a dash of vinegar. Main course (Corfu).

Ψαρι πλακι (**<u>Psah-ree</u> plah-<u>kee</u>**): Fish filled with potato dressed with oil, garlic and other spices is then wrapped and steamed. Main course (Kithira).

Ψαρι χωριατικο (**<u>Psah-ree</u> hoh-ree-<u>ah</u>-tee-koh**): A fish risotto with olive, oregano, tomato, chili, capers. Main course. (Ithaca)

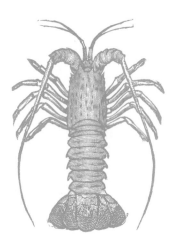

This list contains recipes of some traditional dishes you can try out in your own home. All the ingredients used are available at any supermarket. Wherever typically Greek products are indicated, these can be ordered from a store which imports foodstuffs from all round the world or in Greek or Jewish restaurants.
The recipes serve four.

 Αγκιναρες με κρεας, αυγολεμονο
(Ah-ghee-nah-res meh kreh-ahs av-goh-leh-moh-noh)

Ingredients:

lamb's shoulder	*2 lb*	*(1 kg)*
artichokes	*6*	
baby onions	*2-3*	
butter or margarine	*7 oz*	*(200 gr)*
lemon	*1*	
flour	*2 tablespoons*	
eggs	*2*	
white wine	*½ glass*	
dill, salt, pepper		

Method:

Cut the meat into small cubes and brown them slightly with butter and finely minced onions. Add the artichokes which have been cut in two and prepared. Place them all in an earthenware baking pan and, adding wine and dill, allow to bake in a medium-hot oven for about twenty minutes. Prepare the *av-goh-leh-moh-noh* sauce with two eggs, first whisking the whites till stiff then adding the yolks with lemon juice. Pour the mix into the baking pan and place it in the oven while it is still hot but turned off. Let it set for 15 minutes. Serve hot.

Αρακας με κρεας
(Ah-rah-<u>kas</u> meh <u>kreh</u>-ahs)

Ingredients:

lamb or veal	2 lb	*(1 kg)*
butter	8 oz	*(225 gr)*
peeled tomatoes	4	
kahs-<u>seh</u>-ree *(or Dutch cheese)*	4-5 pieces	
spring peas	1 lb	*(½ kg)*
salt and pepper		

1 puff pastry for bahk-lah-<u>vah</u>
  (or finely cut puff pastry) measuring
  about 16 x 23 in (40 x 60 cm)

Method:

Brown the finely cut meat in butter. Add the chopped spring peas and peeled tomato and allow to cook for ten minutes. Cut the puff pastry into rectangles of about 4¾ inches. on the shorter side. After buttering the surface of the puff pastry, place the stuffing here and roll it over several times. Seal the sides and pour melted butter over it. Cover the rolls with a greaseproof paper before placing them in a hot oven. Baking time, 1 hour.

Αρνι γιουβετσι
(**Ahr-nee** yoo-**vet**-see)

Ingredients:

leg of lamb	*2 lb*	*(1 kg)*
butter or oil	*4 oz*	*(100 gr)*
small soup noodles	*1 lb*	*(¹/₂ kg)*
peeled tomato	*1 lb*	*(¹/₂ kg)*

2 cloves of garlic, salt and pepper

Method:

Cut two slits in the leg of lamb to insert the cloves of garlic. Season with salt, pepper, oil and peeled tomato. Place the meat in the eathenware baking pan and cook in oven for about an hour and a half at medium temperature. Add two cups of boiling water or broth and fill the pot with the small soup noodles. Allow to cook for a further 20 minutes and then serve with grated cheese.

Μελιτζανοσαλατα
(Meh-lit-tsah-noh-sah-<u>lah</u>-tah)

Ingredients:

round eggplants with white pulp	4
olive oil	½ cup
onion	1
vinegar	
salt, pepper	

Method:
Clean the eggplants and slit in two points. Roast them over a low flame or in a barbecue. Allow them to cool, and peel off the burnt skin then place them in a blender. Add oil, onion, vinegar and salt. You will obtain a very fluid cream to spread on fresh or toasted bread. Garnish with *Kah-lah-<u>mah</u>-tah* olives (A Peloponnese specialty).

Μουσακα μελιτζανες
(Moos-sah-<u>kah</u> meh-lit-<u>tsah</u>-nes)

Ingredients:

average-size round eggplants	8	
ragout made from	3 lb	(¹/₂ kg)
minced meat	1 lb	(¹/₂ kg)
and ripe tomatoes	2 lb	(1 kg)
bechamel		
sheep's milk cheese		

Method:

Cut up the eggplants and salt them, then put them aside for half an hour before flouring and frying them. Place in a baking pan and cover with ragout adding another layer of eggplants, then the rest of the ragout. Top the whole with the Greek bechamel (see "Sauces and Condiments"). Finally place in oven at medium heat until the bechamel turns gold colored.

Τζατζικι
(**Zah-<u>zee</u>-kee**)

Ingredients:

Greek yoghurt	*9 oz*	*(250 gr)*
medium-size cucumber	*1*	
clove of garlic	*1*	
mint, salt		
olive oil	*½ cup*	
a drop or two of lemon		

Method:

Remove the skin of the cucumber and chop the latter into
small pieces. Drain out to remove excess water and place in
yoghurt seasoned with oil, chopped garlic, mint, salt and one
or two drops of lemon. Mix delicately to obtain a blend.
Place in refrigerator and serve with fried meat, fish or
vegetable.

Τυροπιτα
(Tee-roh-pee-tah)

Ingredients:
feh-tah *cheese*	*1 lb*	*(¹/₂ kg)*
puff pastry for bak-lah-vah	*1 lb*	*(¹/₂ kg)*
(or frozen puff pastry)		
butter, pepper	*5 oz*	*(150 gr)*
1 whole egg (and 1 yolk if using		
frozen puff pastry)		
some aniseed.		

Method:
Work up the cheese with a fork and soften the pastry with a
little milk. Add the egg and mix well, inserting the aniseed.
Roll out a layer of *bak-lah-vah* pastry (or puff pastry).
Sprinkle a tablespoon of melted butter over the surface then
add another layer of pastry and melted butter and so on until
half the puff pastry is used up. Place the mixture of cheese
over the puff pastry and cover with other layers of pastry
alternating them with melted butter. Place in a hot oven for
20 minutes. If a frozen puff pastry is used, butter is not
needed but don't forget to brush the surface of the puff pastry
with the egg yolk.

Αρνι σουβλακι
(**Ahr**-nee soov-**lah**-kee)

Ingredients:

boned leg of lamb	1
olive oil	½ glass
lemon juice, salt, pepper and oregano	

Method:
Cut the leg into cubes and string them on a spit allowing them to marinate for an hour in oil, lemon, salt, pepper, and oregano. Then cook them over live coals and serve with *zah-zee-kee* sauce, sliced tomato, parsley leaves. They can too eaten in a *pee-tah* or white pizza.

Αρνι φρικασε με μαρουλια
(**Ahr-nee free-kahs-seh** meh mah-**roo**-lee-ah)

Ingredients:

lamb's breast or shoulder	2 lb	(1 kg)
chopped medium-size onion	2	
butter	8 oz	(225 gr)
tablespoons of flour	2	
finely chopped small lettuces	2	
hot water	4 cups	
spoons of salt	2	
teaspoon of pepper	1/2	
parsley or dill	2 oz	(50 gr)
eggs	3	
lemon juice		

Method:

Brown the meat and the onion in butter. Sprinkle with flour
and mix well. Add the lettuce leaves, hot water, salt and
pepper. Add dill and allow to cook in a pot with a lid for
about an hour over a low heat. Remove from heat and
prepare the *av-goh-leh-moh-noh* sauce: whisk the whites of
the eggs and continue whisking after pouring in the yolks
and lemon. Dilute the sauce with half a cup of broth of the
meat that has just been cooked. Slowly pour the sauce over
the meat and serve hot.

RECIPES

Αμυγδαλωτα Υδραϊκα
(Ah-mig-thah-loh-<u>tah</u> Ee-<u>dreh</u>-ee-kah)

Ingredients:

peeled almonds	1 lb	(¹/₂ kg)
sugar	9 oz	(250 gr)
tablespoons of semolina	5	
icing sugar	1 lb	(¹/₂ kg)
of orange blossom water	1 ¹/₂ cups	
cloves		
butter to grease the baking pan		

Method:

Whip up the almonds with two tablespoons of sugar. Add the
rest of the sugar, the semolina and 6 spoonfuls of orange
blossom water. Mix to a soft blend and add orange blossom
water if it is still too thick. Make pear-shaped balls (the size
of a walnut) the tail of which will be represented by a clove.
Place in butter-greased and floured baking pan and bake at a
low temperature for 20 minutes. When cool, immerse in
orange blossom water and dip each piece into icing sugar.

Ζαχαροπουλια Λεσβου
(Zah-ha-roh-<u>poo</u>-lee-ah <u>Les</u>-voo)

Ingredients:

sugar	*8 oz*	*(225 gr)*
almost a cup of water	*7 oz*	*(200 gr)*
peeled and ground almonds	*1 lb*	*(450 gr)*
ground mastica	*½ teaspoon*	
icing sugar		

Method:

Boil the water and sugar for ten minutes. Add the almonds and let it all thicken over a low flame, stirring continuously. Remove from heat, add the mastic and stir until the mixture cools down. With hands covered with icing sugar, sculpt the marzipan paste into shapes of birds or fruit or flowers. Cover the sweets with icing sugar.

Χαλβας Σιμιγδαλι
(Hahl-vahs see-mig-dah-lee)

Ingredients:

butter	8 oz	(225 gr)
nuts or pine nuts	2 tablespoonfuls	
peeled almonds	2 tablespoonfuls	
large-grain semolina	9 oz	(250 gr)
sugar	1 lb oz	(500 gr)
cinnamon sticks	2	
cloves	2 or 3	
powdered cinnamon		
boiling milk	2 cups	

Method:

Melt the butter in a pot and add the semolina. Cook over a low heat stirring continually. As soon as the mix turns golden, add the pine seeds (or the nuts), almonds, cinnamon and cloves. Continue stirring, then add sugar and the boiling milk. Cook for a minute or so until the liquid is completely absorbed in the mix. Remove from the heat and pour the mixture into a mold. Cover with a cloth and let it rest for a few minutes. Turn out onto a dish and garnish it with almonds and sprinkle powdered cinnamon over the pudding.

In case you need to spell in Greek, here are the letters of the alphabet together with their phonetic pronunciation:

α, A	αλφα <u>ahl</u>-fah	ν, N	νι <u>nee</u>
β, B	βητα <u>vee</u>-tah	ξ, Ξ	ξι <u>ksee</u>
γ, Γ	γαμα <u>gah</u>-mah	o, O	ομικρον <u>oh</u>-mee-kron
δ, Δ	δελτα <u>del</u>-tah	π, Π	πι <u>pee</u>
ε, E	εψιλον <u>ep</u>-see-lon	ρ, P	ρο roh
ζ, Z	ζητα <u>zee</u>-tah	σ, Σ	σιγμα <u>sig</u>-mah
η, H	ητα <u>ee</u>-tah	τ, T	ταυ tahf
θ, Θ	θητα <u>thee</u>-tah	υ, Y	υψιλον <u>eep</u>-see-lon
ι, I	ιοτα <u>yoh</u>-tah	φ, Φ	φι fee
κ, K	καπα <u>kahp</u>-pah	χ, X	χι hee
λ, Λ	λαμδα <u>lahm</u>-dah	ψ, Ψ	ψι psee
μ, M	μι mee	ω, Ω	ωμεγα oh-<u>meh</u>-gah

I have a small child/ two children	Εχω ενα μωρο/ δυο παιδακια *eh-ho eh-nah moh-roh/dee-oh peh-dah-kee-ah*
Do you have discounts for children?	Κανετε σκοντο για παιδια; *kahn-eh-teh skon-toh yah peh-dee-ah?*
Do you have a small bed for the child?	Εχετε κρεβατακι για το μωρο; *eh-heh-teh kreh-vah-tah-kee yah toh moh-roh?*
Do you have a menu for children?	Εχετε μενου για παιδια; *eh-heh-teh meh-noo yah peh-dee-ah?*
Can you warm up the feeding bottle for the child?	Μπορειτε να ζεστανετε το μπιμπερον; *boh-ree-teh nah zehs-tah-neh-teh toh bee-beh-ron?*
Where can I feed/ change the child?	Που μπορω να το ταισω/ να αλλαξω το μωρο; *poo boh-roh nah toh tah-iss-soh/ nah al-lak-so toh moh-roh?*
Do you have a high chair?	Εχετε ενα καρεκλακι; *eh-heh-teh eh-na kah-reh-klah-kee?*
Is there a garden where the children can play?	Υπαρχει κηπος για να παιζουν τα παιδια; *ee-par-hee kee-pohs yah nah peh-zoon tah peh-dee-ah?*
Please will you bring me a glass of water at room temperature?	Σας παρακαλω, μου φερνετε ενα ποτηρι νερο θερμοκρασιας δωματιου; *sahs pah-rah-kah-loh, moo fer-neh-teh eh-nah poh-tee-ree neh-roh ther-moh-krahs-see-ahs doh-mah-tee-oo?*

This doesn't work	Αυτο δεν λειτουργει *ahf-toh den lee-toor-gee*
It has a flaw	Ειναι ελαττωματικο *ee-neh eh-lah-toh-mah-tee-koh*
We are still waiting to be served	Ακομη, περιμενουμε να μας σερβιρετε *ah-koh-mee, peh-ree-meh-noo-meh* *nah mahs ser-vee-reh-teh*
The coffee is cold	Ο καφες ειναι κρυος *oh kah-fehs ee-neh kree-os*
This meat is tough	Αυτο το κρεας ειναι πολυ σκληρο *ahf-toh toh kreh-ahs ee-neh poh-lee* *sklee-roh*
The tablecloth is not clean	Το τραπεζομαντηλο δεν ειναι καθαρο *toh trah-peh-zoh-mah-dee-loh den* *ee-neh kah-thah-roh*
The room is noisy	Το δωματιο ειναι θορυβωδες *toh doh-mah-tee-oh ee-neh thoh-ree-* *voh-des*
There's too much smoke here	Εδω εχει πολυ καπνο *eh-doh eh-hee poh-lee kahp-noh*

Do you speak English?	Μιλατε αγγλικα *mee-lah-teh ah-glee-kah*
I don't speak Greek	Δεν μιλω ελληνικα *den mee-loh ell-ee-nee-kah*
What's your name? (formal/informal)	Πως σας λενε/ Πως σε λενε; *pohs-sas leh-neh? pohs seh leh-neh?*
My name is …	Με λενε... *meh leh-neh …*
Do you mind if I sit here?	Σας πειραζει αν καθησω εδω; *sahs pee-rat-zee ahn kah-thees-soh eh-doh?*
Is this seat free?	Ειναι ελευθερο αυτο το καθησμα; *ee-neh eh-lef-theh-roh ahf-toh toh kah-thiz-mah?*
Where do you come from?	Απο που εισθε; *ah-poh poo ees-teh?*
I come from...	Ειμαι απο... *ee-meh ah-poh …*
I am British/ American	Ειμαι αγγλος/αμερικαυός *ee-meh ah-glohs/ah-meh-ree-kah-nohs*
Can I buy you a coffee? / something to drink?	Μπορω να σας κερασω ενα καφε/ κατι να πιητε; *boh-roh nah sahs keh-rahs-soh eh-na kahf-feh/kah-tee nah pyee-teh?*

First of March	πρωτη Μαρτιου _proh-tee mahr-tee-oo_	
Second of June	δυο Ιουνιου _dee-oh ee-oo-nee-oo_	
We will arrive on the 29th of August	Θα φθασουμε στις 29 Αυγουστου _thah fthahs-soo-meh stiss_ _ee-kos-see-eh-neh-ah av-goos-too_	
Nineteen- ninety-seven	Δεκαεννεα Εννενηντα επτα _the-kah-eh-neh-ah eh-neh-nee_ _dah eh-ptah_	
Monday	Δευτερα	_def-teh-rah_
Tuesday	Τριτη	_tree-tee_
Wednesday	Τεταρτη	_teh-tahr-tee_
Thursday	Πεμπτη	_pehm-tee_
Friday	Παρασκευη	_pah-rahs-keh-vee_
Saturday	Σαββατο	_sah-vah-toh_
Sunday	Κυριακη	_kee-ree-ah-kee_
January	Ιανουαριος	_ee-ah-noo-ah-ree-ohs_
February	Φεβρουαριος	_fev-roo-ah-ree-os_
March	Μαρτιος	_mahr-tee-ohs_
April	Απριλιος	_ah-pree-lee-ohs_
May	Μαιος	_mah-ee-ohs_
June	Ιουνιος	_ee-oo-nee-ohs_
July	Ιουλιος	_ee-oo-lee-ohs_
August	Αυγουστος	_av-goos-tos_
September	Σεπτεμβριος	_sep-tem-vree-ohs_
October	Οκτωβριος	_ok-tov-ree-ohs_
November	Νοεμβριος	_noh-em-vree-ohs_
December	Δεκεμβριος	_deh-kem-vree-ohs_

Pardon me, where's the railway station?	Συγνωμη, που ειναι ο σταθμος των τραινων; *sig-noh-mee, poo ee-neh oh stath-moss ton treh-non?*
How do I get to the airport?	Πως πανε στο αεροδρομιο; *pos pah-neh stoh ah-er-oh-droh-mee-oh?*
Can you tell me the way to the station?	Μπορειτε να μου δειξετε το δρομο για το σταθμο; *boh-ree-teh nah moo deeks-eh-teh toh droh-moh yah toh stahth-moh?*
Is this the way to the Acropolis?	Απο δω πανε στην Ακροπολη; *ah-poh doh pah-neh stin ah-kroh-poh-lee*
I'm looking for the Tourist Information Office	Ζητω το γραφειο πληροφορειων για τουριστες *zee-toh toh grah-fee-oh plee-roh-foh-ree-on yah too-rees-tes*
Which road do I take for ... ?	Ποιο δρομο πρεπει να παρω για...; *pee-oh droh-moh pre-pee nah pah-ro yah ... ?*
How long will it take to get there?	Ποση ωρα κανει να φθασει; *pos-see oh-rah kah-nee nah fthas-see?*
Pardon me, can you tell me where the restaurant ... is?	Συγνωμη, ξερετε που ειναι το εστιατοριο...; *sig-noh-mee, kseh-reh-teh poo ee-neh toh es-tee-ah-toh-ree-oh ...?*

Things to remember

> Greek bars are more of a cafeteria-type of place where
> people sit down to eat and drink. You may ask for only a
> simple coffee (obviously Greek) or something else like a
> soft drink, pastries, and sweets in general. In recent years
> Italian espresso and cappuccino coffee are also served.
> Normally, the bill is paid after you have finished and not
> when you give your order.

A coffee/a cappuccino	Ενα καφε *ee-nah kaf-feh/kah-poot-see-noh*
A draught beer	Μια μπυρα βαρελισια *mee-ah bir-rah vah-reh-lee-see-ah*
An ale/porter/ medium	Μια μπυρα ξανθη/ σκουρη/ μετρια *mee-ah bir-rah ksan-thee/skoo-ree/meh-tree-ah*
Two cups of tea with milk	Δυο τσϊ με γαλα *dee-oh tsah-ee meh gah-lah*
A glass of mineral water	Ενα ποτηρι μεταλλικο νερο *ee-nah poh-tee-ree meh-tah-lee-koh neh-roh*
With ice, please	Με παγακι, σας παρακαλω *meh pah-gah-kee, sahs pah-rah-kah-loh*
Some more coffee, please	Σας παρακαλω, ακομη ενα καφε *sahs pah-rah-kah-loh ah-koh-mee eh-nah kahf-feh*
May I have the bill, please?	Μου φερνετε τον λογαριασμο, παρακαλω; *moo fer-neh-teh ton loh-gah-ree-az-moh, pah-rah-kah-loh?*

Good evening, we'd like a table for two	Καλησπερα, θα θελαμε ενα τραπεζι για δυο *kah-lis-peh-rah, thah theh-lah-meh eh-nah trah-peh-zee ya dee-oh*
We'd like a table in a quiet corner	Θα θελαμε ενα τραπεζι στη γωνια, ησυχο *thah theh-lah-meh eh-nah trah-peh-zee stee goh-nee-ah, ees-see-hoh*
We booked a table for two in the name of …	Εχουμε κλεισει τραπεζι για δυο, στο ονομα... *eh-hoo-meh klees-see trah-peh-zee yah dee-oh stoh oh-noh-mah …*
Can we eat outside?	Μπορουμε να καθησουμε εξω; *boh-roo-meh nah kah-thees-soo-meh eks-hoh?*
We'd like a table far from/near the window	Θα θελαμε ενα τραπεζι μακρια απο το/κοντα στο παραθυρο *thah theh-lah-meh eh-na trah-peh-zee mah-kree-ah ah-poh toh/kon-dah stoh pah-rah-thee-roh*
Is there an entrance for the disabled?	Υπαρχει εισοδος για αναπηρους; *ee-pahr-hee ees-soh-dos yah ah-nah-pee-roos?*
Do you have a fixed-price menu?	Εχετε μενου με καθορισμενη τιμη; *eh-heh-teh meh-noo meh kah-thoh-ris-meh-nee tee-mee?*
Do we have to wait long?	Θα περιμενουμε πολυ; *thah peh-ree-meh-noo-meh poh-lee?*
Where is the cloak-room?	Που ειναι η γκουαρδαρομπα; *poo ee-neh ee goo-ar-dah-roh-bah?*

May we see the menu?	Μπορουμε να δουμε το μενου; *boh-<u>roo</u>-meh nah <u>doo</u>-meh* *toh meh-<u>noo</u>?*
Do you have a vegetarian menu?	Εχετε μενου χορτοφαγων; *<u>eh</u>-heh-teh meh-<u>noo</u> hor-toh-<u>fah</u>-gon?*
What is the specialty of the house?	Ποια ειναι η σπεσιαλιτε του σπιτιου; *pee-<u>ah</u> ee-neh ee spes-see-ah-lee-<u>teh</u>* *too spee-tee-<u>oo</u>?*
What is the dish of the day?	Ποιο ειναι το πιατο της ημερας; *pee-<u>oh</u> ee-neh toh pee-<u>ah</u>-toh tis* *ee-<u>meh</u>-rahs?*
What's in this dish?	Τι εχει μεσα αυτο το πιατο; *tee eh-<u>hee</u> <u>mes</u>-sah ahf-<u>toh</u> toh* *pee-<u>ah</u>-toh?*
Is it spicy?	Ειναι καυτερο; *ee-neh kahf-teh-<u>roh</u>?*
I'm allergic to bell peppers	Ειμαι αλλεργικος στη πιπερια *<u>ee</u>-meh al-ler-gee-<u>kos</u> stee* *pee-peh-ree-<u>ah</u>*
Is there garlic/ pepper in this dish?	Αυτο το πιατο εχει σκορδο/ πιπερι; *ahf-<u>toh</u> toh pee-<u>ah</u>-toh eh-<u>hee</u>* *<u>skor</u>-doh/ pee-<u>peh</u>-ree?*
We would like to try ...	Θελουμε να δοκιμασουμε... *<u>theh</u>-loo-meh nah dok-ee-<u>mas</u>-soo-* *meh ...*
We would like some more bread, please	Μας φερνετε κιαλλο ψωμι, σας παρακαλω *mas <u>fer</u>-neh-teh kee-<u>al</u>-loh psoh-<u>mee</u>,* *sahs parah-kah-<u>loh</u>*

Do you have … ?
Εχετε...;
eh-heh-teh … ?

I would/we would like …
Θα ηθελα/ θα θελαμε...
thah ee-theh-lah / thah theh-lah-meh …

Can you bring me/ us … ?
Μου/ μας φερνετε...
moo/ mahs fer-neh-teh …

I would like a portion/half a portion of …
Θα ηθελα μια μεριδα/ μιση μεριδα...
thah ee-theh-lah mee-ah meh-ree-dah/mis-see meh-ree-dah …

What are the typical dishes of the region?
Ποια ειναι τα χαρακτηριστικα φαγητα της περιοχης;
pee-ah ee-neh tah hah-rak-tee-ris-tee-kah fah-gee-tah tis peh-ree-oh-hees?

Which is the typical local cheese?
Ποιο ειναι το τυρι του τοπου;
pee-oh ee-neh toh tee-ree too toh-poo

What desserts/fruit do you have ?
Τι γλυκα/ φρουτα εχετε;
tee glee-kah/ froot-tah eh-heh-teh ?

We'd like a portion of …with two plates
Θα θελαμε μια μεριδα... με δυο πιατα
thah theh-lah-meh mee-ah meh-ree-dah … meh dee-oh pee-ah-tah

Four coffees, please
Τεσσερις καφεδες, παρακαλω
tes-seh-ris kah-feh-des, pah-rah-kah-loh

Can you bring me the bill, please?
Μου φερνετε το λογαριασμο, παρακαλω;
moo fer-neh-teh toh loh-gah-ree-ahs-moh pah-rah-kah-loh?

Waiter!	Κυριε! *kee-ree-eh!*
Is there a coat-stand?	Υπαρχει μια κρεμαστρα; *ee-pahr-hee mee-ah kreh-mahs-trah?*
Can you turn on the fan?	Μπορειτε να βαλλετε τον ανεμιστηρα; *boh-ree-teh nah vah-leh-teh ton ah-neh-mis-tee-rah?*
Could you bring me some breadsticks, please?	Μου φερνετε γκριτσινια, σας παρακαλω *moo fer-neh-teh grit-see-nee-ah, sahs pah-rah-kah-loh?*
What drinks do you have?	Τι ποτα/ τι αναψυκτικα εχετε; *tee poh-tah/ tee ah-nahp-sik-tee-kah eh-heh-teh?*
What brands of beer do you have in stock?	Τι μαρκα μπυρα εχετε; *tee mar-kah bir-rah eh-heh-teh?*
A quarter liter of the home brew, please	Ενα τεταρτο κρασι χυμα, σας παρακαλω *eh-nah teh-tar-toh krahs-see hee-mah, sahs pah-rah-kah-loh*
Where is the appetizers buffet?	Που ειναι το τραπεζι με τα ορεκτικα; *Poo ee-neh toh trah-peh-zee meh tah oh-rehk-tee-kah?*
Is the fish fresh/ frozen?	Το ψαρι ειναι φρεσκο/ κατεψυγμενο; *toh psah-ree ee-neh fres-koh/kah-tep- sig-meh-noh?*
Does this come with a side dish?	Αυτο το πιατο εχει και γαρνιτουρες; *ahf-toh toh pee-ah-toh eh-hee keh gar-nee-too-res?*

Can we have mixed side dishes?	Γινεται να εχουμε ποικιλια γαρνιτουρες; *gee-neh-teh nah <u>eh</u>-hoo-meh pee-kee-<u>lee</u>-ah gahr-nee-<u>too</u>-res?*
I'd like it cooked with little salt	Θα το ηθελα με πολυ λιγο αλατι *thah toh ee-theh-lah meh poh-<u>lee</u> <u>lee</u>-goh ah-<u>lah</u>-tee*
I'd like the meat rare/medium/ well done	Θα ηθελα το κρεας με το αιμα/ πολυ λιγο ψημενο/ πολυ ψημενο *thah <u>ee</u>-the-lah toh <u>kreh</u>-ahs meh toh <u>eh</u>-mah/ poh-<u>lee</u> <u>lee</u>-goh psee-<u>meh</u>-noh/poh-<u>lee</u> psee-<u>meh</u>-noh*
Can you heat this up, please?	Μου την ζεσταινετε, αν εχετε την καλωσυνη; *moo tin zes-<u>teh</u>-neh-teh, ahn eh-heh-teh tin kah-los-<u>see</u>-nee?*
This isn't the dish I ordered.	Δεν παρηγγειλα αυτο το πιατο *den pah-<u>ree</u>-gee-lah ahf-<u>toh</u> toh pee-<u>ah</u>-toh*
Could you pass me the salt/oil, please?	Μου δινετε το αλατι/ το λαδι, σας παρακαλω; *moo <u>dee</u>-neh-teh toh ah-<u>lah</u>-tee/ toh <u>lah</u>-dee, sahs pah-rah-kah-<u>loh</u>?*
Do you have ice-cream?	Εχετε παγωτα; *<u>eh</u>-heh-teh pah-goh-<u>tah</u>?*
I'd like a sweet/dry sparkling wine	Θα ηθελα μια σαμπανια γλυκυ/ ξηρη *thah <u>ee</u>-theh-lah mee-<u>ah</u> sahm-<u>pah</u>-nee-ah glee-<u>kee</u>/ksee-<u>ree</u>*
A digestive, thank you	Ενα ποτο πεπτικο, ευχαριστω *<u>eh</u>-nah poh-<u>toh</u> pep-tee-<u>koh</u>, ef-hah-ris-<u>toh</u>*

May I book a table for four?	Ειναι δυνατον να κλεισουμε τραπεζι για τεσσερις; _ee-neh dee-nah-<u>ton</u> nah <u>klees</u>-soo-meh trah-<u>peh</u>-zee yah <u>tes</u>-seh-ris?_
I would like to book a table for two for this evening/ tomorrow evening at eight, in the name of …	Θα ηθελα να κλεισω τραπεζι για δυο ατομα, για αποψε/αυριο βραδυ, στις οκτω, στο ονομα... _thah <u>ee</u>-theh-lah nah <u>klees</u>-soh trah-<u>peh</u>-zee yah <u>dee</u>-oh <u>ah</u> toh-mah, yah ah-<u>pop</u>-seh/<u>avree</u>-oh <u>vrah</u>-dee, stis ok-<u>toh</u>, stoh <u>oh</u>-noh-mah …_
On which day of the week is it closed?	Ποια ημερα της εβδομαδος ειναι κλειστο; _pee-<u>ah</u> ee-<u>meh</u>-rah tis ev-doh-<u>mah</u>-dos <u>ee</u>-neh klis-<u>toh</u>?_
What time does the restaurant open/close?	Τι ωρα ανοιγει/κλεινει το ριστοραν; _tee <u>oh</u>-rah ah-<u>nee</u>-gee/<u>klee</u>-nee toh ris-toh-<u>rahn</u>?_
I'd like to cancel a booking I made for this evening, for two in the name of…	Θα ηθελα να ακηρωσω μια κρατηση που ειχα κανει για αποψε, για δυο ατομα, στο ονομα... _thah <u>ee</u>-theh-lah nah ah-kee-<u>ros</u>-soh <u>mee</u>-ah <u>krah</u>-tis-see poo ee-hah <u>kah</u>-nee yah ah-<u>pop</u>-seh, yah <u>dee</u>-oh <u>ah</u>-toh-mah, stoh <u>oh</u>-noh-mah …_
Is it necessary to reserve?	Ειναι απαραιτητη η κρατηση; _ee-neh ah-pah-<u>reh</u>-tee-tee ee <u>krah</u>-tis-see?_

We'd like an aperitif Θα θελαμε ενα απεριτιφ
thah theh-lah-meh eh-nah ah-per-it-if

What wine would
you suggest with
this dish?
Τι κρασι μας συστηνετε με αυτο το
πιατο;
*tee krahs-see mahs sis-tee-neh-teh meh
ahf-toh toh pee-ah-toh?*

Can you
recommend
a good white/rosé/
red wine?
Μπορειτε να μας συμβουλευσετε ενα
καλο ασπρο κρασι/ κοκινο/ ροζε;
*boh-ree-teh nah mahs sim-voo
lef-seh-teh eh-nah kah-loh ahs-
proh krahs-see/ koh-kee-noh/ roh-zeh?*

Can you bring us
the house wine,
please?
Μας φερνετε κρασι του σπιτιου,
παρακαλω;
*mahs fer-neh-teh krahs-see too
spee-tee-oo, pah-rah-kah-loh?*

A botte /A half
bottle of …
Μια/ μιση μποτιλια...
mee-ah/mis-see bot-tee-lee-ah

A bottle of natural/
sparkling mineral
water, please
Παρακαλω, μια μποτιλια μεταλικο
νερο/ φυσικο/ ανθρακουχο
*pah-rah-kah-loh, mee-ah bot-tee-lee-ah
meh-tah-lee-koh neh-roh/fis-see-
koh/ahn-trah-koo-hoh*

Can you bring us
another bottle of
water/wine, please?
Σας παρακαλουμε, μας φερνετε ενα
αλλο μπουκαλι νερο/ κρασι
*sahs pah-rah-kah-loo-meh, mahs fer-
neh-teh eh-nah ahl-loh boo-kah-lee
neh-ro/krahs-see?*

Is there a good restaurant in this area?	Υπαρχει καλο εστιατοριο στην περιοχη; *ee-pahr-hee kah-loh es-tee-ah toh-ree-oh stin peh-ree-oh-hee?*
Is there an inexpensive restaurant near here?	Υπαρχει φθηνο εστιατοριο εδω κοντα; *ee-pahr-hee fthee-noh es-tee-ah-toh-ree-oh eh-doh kon-dah?*
Do you know of a restaurant with typical local cooking?	Μπορειτε να μου υποδειξετε ενα εστιατοριο με ελληνικη κουζινα; *boh-ree-teh nah moo ee-poh-dix-eh-teh eh-nah es-tee-ah-toh-ree-oh meh eh-lee-nee-kee koo-zee-nah?*
How do I get there?	Πως πανε εκει; *pohs pah-neh eh-kee?*
Excuse me, can you tell me where the ... restaurant is?	Με συγχωρειτε, ξερετε που ειναι το εστιατοριο...; *meh sin-goh-ree-teh, kseh-reh-teh poo ee-neh toh es-tee-ah-toh-ree-oh... ?*
What's the best restaurant in the city?	Ποιο ειναι το καλυτερο εστιατοριο της πολεως; *pee-oh ee-neh toh kah-lee-teh-roh es-tee-ah-toh-ree-oh tis poh-leh-os?*
We would like to have a meal in a restaurant which is not too expensive	Θα θελαμε να φαμε σε ενα ριστοραν οχι ακριβο *thah theh-lah-meh nah fah-meh seh eh-nah ris-to-rahnt oh-hee ahk-ree-voh*

Is there a telephone here?	Εχει τηλεφωνο εδω; *eh-hee tee-<u>leh</u>-foh-noh eh-<u>doh</u>?*
Excuse me, where's the restroom?	Που ειναι η τουαλετα, παρακαλω; *poo <u>ee</u>-neh ee too-ah-<u>leh</u>-tah, pah-rah-kah-<u>loh</u>?*
Could you bring me another glass/plate?	Μπορειτε να μου φερετε ενα αλλο ποτηρι/ πιατο; *boh-<u>ree</u>-teh nah moo <u>feh</u>-reh-teh <u>eh</u>-nah <u>ah</u>-loh poh-<u>tee</u>-ree/pee-<u>aht</u>-toh?*
Could you change my fork/ knife/ spoon, please?	Μου αλλαζετε το πηρουνι/ το μαχαιρι/ το κουταλι παρακαλω; *moo ahl-<u>lah</u>-zeh-teh toh pee-<u>roo</u>-nee/toh mah-<u>heh</u>-ree/toh koo-<u>tah</u>-lee pah-rah-kah-<u>loh</u>?*
Can you turn the heating up/down?	Μπορειτε να χαμηλωσετε/ δυναμωσετε το καλοριφερ; *boh-<u>ree</u>-teh nah hah-mee-<u>lohs</u>-seh-teh/dee-nah-<u>moh</u>-seh-teh toh kah-loh-ree-<u>fer</u>?*
Can you open/close the window?	Μπορειτε να ανοιξετε/ να κλεισετε το παραθυρο; *boh-<u>ree</u> teh-nah ah-<u>neex</u>-eh-teh/nah <u>klees</u>-seh-teh toh pah-<u>rah</u>-thee-roh?*
I've stained myself, do you have some talcum powder?	Λερωθηκα, εχετε ταλκ; *leh-<u>roh</u>-thee-kah, <u>eh</u>-heh-teh tahlk?*
What time do you close?	Τι ωρα κλεινετε; *tee <u>oh</u>-rah <u>klee</u>-neh-teh?*

Which appetizers do you have?

Τι ορεκτικα εχετε;
tee oh-rehk-tee-<u>kah</u> <u>eh</u>-heh-teh?

What ingredients are there in this wrapped-and-steamed fish?

Τι συστατικα εχει αυτο το ψαρι στη λαδοκολα;
tee- sis-tah-tee-<u>kah</u> <u>eh</u>-hee ahf-<u>toh</u> toh <u>psah</u>-ree stee lah-<u>doh</u>-koh-lah?

I would like a *tee-<u>roh</u>-pee-tah* with mixed salad

Θα ηθελα μια τυροπιτα με μια χωριατικη σαλατα
thah <u>ee</u>-theh-lah <u>mee</u>-ah tee-<u>roh</u>-pee-tah meh <u>mee</u>-ah hoh-ree-<u>ah</u>-tee-kee sah-<u>lah</u>-tah

I would like a complete *soov-lah-kee*

Ενα σουβλακι με απ'ολα
<u>eh</u>-nah soo-<u>vlah</u>-kee meh ah-<u>poh</u>-lah

Can you change the ... with the ...?

Μπορειτε να μου φερετε... αντι για...
boh-<u>ree</u>-teh nah moo <u>feh</u>-reh-teh... ah-<u>dee</u> yah ...?

We would like a portion of mixed sea-food, thanks

Θα ηθελα μια μεριδα με θαλασσινα διαφορα. Ευχαριστω
thah <u>ee</u>-theh-lah <u>mee</u>-ah meh-<u>ree</u>-dah meh thah-lahs-see-<u>nah</u> dee-<u>ah</u>-foh-rah. ef-hah-ris-<u>toh</u>

Please, only a little oil/ no onions

Πολυ λιγο λαδι, σας παρακαλω/ διχως κρεμμυδι
poh-<u>lee</u> <u>lee</u>-goh <u>lah</u>-dee sahs pah-rah-kah-<u>loh</u>/<u>dee</u>-hos kreh-<u>mee</u>-dee

A Coke/A chilled fruit juice at room temperature

Μια κοκα/ ενα χυμο φρουτου παγωμενο/ οχι κρυο
<u>mee</u>-ah <u>koh</u>-kah/ <u>eh</u>-nah hee-<u>moh</u> froo-too pah-goh-<u>meh</u>-noh/<u>oh</u>-hee <u>kree</u>-oh

Is there a doctor here?	Υπαρχει ενας γιατρος εδω; *ee-pahr-hee eh-nahs ee-ah-tros eh-doh?*
Call a doctor/ an ambulance!	Καλεστε εναν γιατρο/ ενα ασθενοφορο! *kah-les-teh eh-nahn ee-ah-troh/ eh-nah ahs-theh-noh-foh-roh!*
Go and get help, quick!	Πηγαινετε να ζητησετε βοηθεια, γρηγορα! *pee-geh-neh-teh nah zee-tees-seh-teh voh-ee-thee-ah, gree-goh-rah!*
My wife's about to have a baby	Η γυναικα μου ειναι ετοιμη για να γεννησει *ee gee-neh-kah moo ee-neh eh-tee-mee yah nah geh-nees-see*
Where is the nearest police station/ hospital?	Που ειναι μια αστυνομια/ το πιο κοντινο νοσοκομειο; *poo ee-neh mee-ah ahs-tee-noh-mee-ah/ toh pee-oh kon-dee-noh nos-soh-koh-mee-oh?*
I've lost my credit card/my wallet	Εχασα την πιστωτικη μου καρτα/ το πορτοφολι μου *eh-hahs-sah tin pis-toh-tee-kee moo kar-tah/ toh por-toh-foh-lee moo*
I've been robbed	Με εχουν κατακλεψει *meh-hoon kah-tah-klep-see*
They've stolen my wallet	Μου εκλεψαν το πορτοφολι *moo eh-klep-sahn toh por-toh-foh-lee*
I've lost my son/ my bag	Εχασα το γιο μου/ την τσαντα μου *eh-hahs-sah toh ee-oh moo/ teen tsahn-dah moo*

Are there any night clubs?	Υπαρχουν νυκτερινα κεντρα; *ee-pahr-hoon nik-ter-ee-nah ken-drah?*
Is there any place/show for children?	Υπαρχει κανενα μερος/θεαμα για παιδια; *ee-pahr-hee kah-neh-nah meh-ros/theh-ah-mah yah peh-dee-ah?*
What can one do in the evening?	Που μπορουμε να βγουμε το βραδυ; *poo boh-roo-meh nah vgoo-meh toh vrah-dee?*
Where is there a cinema / a theater?	Που ειναι κανενα σινεμα/ θεατρο; *poo ee-neh kah-neh-nah see-neh-mah/ ee theh-ah-troh?*
Can you book us some seats?	Μπορειτε να μας κλεισετε θεσεις; *boh-ree-teh nah mahs klee-seh-teh theh-sis?*
Is there a swimming pool?	Υπαρχει πισινα; *ee-pahr-hee piss-ee-nah?*
Are there good tours to take?	Εχει ωραιες εκδρομες να κανουμε; *eh-hee ohr-eh-ehs ek-droh-mes nah kah-noo-meh?*
Where can we play tennis?/ golf?	Που μπορουμε να παιξουμε τενις/γκολφ; *poo boh-roo-meh nah pehx-oo-meh teh-nis?/golf?*
Can one go horse-riding?/ fishing?	Ειναι δυνατον να παμε για ιππασια/ για ψαρεμα; *ee-neh din-ah-tohn nah pah-meh yah ee-pahs-see-ah? /yah psah-reh-mah?*

EXPRESSIONS

Good morning	**Καλημερα** *Kah-lee-meh-rah*
Good evening	**Καλησπερα** *Kah-lees-peh-rah*
Good night	**Καληνυκτα** *kah-lee-neek-tah*
See you soon	**Γεια σας** *yah sahs*
How do you do/ Hi!	**Χαιρω πολυ** *heh-roh poh-lee*
How are you?	**Πως εισθε;** *pohs ees-theh?*
Fine, thank you	**Καλα, ευχαριστω** *kah-lah ef-hah-ris-toh*
Please	**Σας παρακαλω** *sas pah-rah-kah-loh*
Excuse me	**Με συγχωρειτε** *meh sin-hoh-ree-teh*
I'm sorry	**Λυπουμαι** *lee-poo-meh*
Yes thank you/ No thank you	**Ναι ευχαριστω/ οχι ευχαριστω** *ne ef-hah-ris-toh/oh-hee ef-hah-ris-toh*
Thanks	**Ευχαριστω** *ef-hah-ris-toh*
I would like/ we would like	**Θα ηθελα/ θα θελαμε...** *thah ee-theh-lah/ thah theh-lah-meh*

GOURMET SHOPPING

Things to remember

> If you wish to buy some Greek delicacies, the best stores
> to go to are the so-called «pahn-toh-poh-lee-oh»
> (delicatessen) where you will be allowed to taste the
> wares before purchasing the specialties. Wines, liqueurs,
> oil, cheese and yoghurt, at low cost and of good quality,
> can be bought in the big supermarkets.

Is this cheese fresh?	Ειναι φρεσκο αυτο το τυρι; _ee-neh fres-koh af-toh toh tee-ree?_
Is this wine sweet?	Εθιναι γλυκο αυτο το κρασι; _ee-neh glee-koh af-toh toh krahs-see?_
What is the price per kilo?	Ποσο κοστιζει το κιλο; _pohs-soh kos-tee-zee toh kee-loh?_
How long will it stay good?	Ποσο καιρο διατηρειται; _pohs-soh keh-roh thee-ah-tee-ree-teh?_
I'll take this/that	Παιρνω αυτο/ εκεινο _per-noh af-toh/ eh-kee-noh_
I'd like two bottles of it.	Θα ηθελα δυο μπουκαλια _thah ee-theh-lah dee-oh boo-kah-lee-ah_
Give me half a kilo	Δωστε μου μισο κιλο _dos-teh moo miss-oh kee-loh_
Can you wrap it for me for the trip?	Μπορειτε να μου το πακεταρετε για ταξιδι; _boh-ree-teh nah moo toh pah-keh-tah-reh-teh yah tah-ksee-dee?_
Is it far?	Ειναι μακρια; _ee-neh mah-kree-ah?_
Does it cost much?	Κοστιζει πολυ; _koss-steet-see poh-lee?_

NOUNS

Nouns in the Greek language vary their form according to number and case. The list below provides you with the most frequent cases and, therefore, the most useful: the nominative, genitive and accusative, with examples of masculine, feminine and neuter gender nouns. They are declined in the singular and the plural, and all preceded by the definite article.

SINGULAR

masculine	feminine	neuter
ο πατερας	η μητερα	το παιδι
oh pah-<u>teh</u>-ras	*ee mee-<u>teh</u>-rah*	*toh peh-<u>dee</u>*
the father	the mother	the child
του πατερα	της μητερας	του παιδιου
too pah-<u>teh</u>-ra	*tis mee-<u>teh</u>-ras*	*too peh-dee-<u>oo</u>*
of the father	of the mother	of the child
τον πατερα	την μητερα	το παιδι
ton pah-<u>teh</u>-rah	*tin mee-<u>teh</u>-rah*	*toh peh-<u>dee</u>*
the father	the mother	the child

PLURAL

masculine	feminine	neuter
οι πατερες	οι μητερες	τα παιδια
ee pah-<u>teh</u>-res	*ee mee-<u>teh</u>-res*	*tah peh-dee-<u>ah</u>*
fathers	mothers	children

των πατερων	των μητερων	των παιδιων
ton pah-<u>teh</u>-ron	*ton mit-<u>teh</u>-ron*	*ton peh-dee-<u>on</u>*
of the fathers	of the mothers	of the children

τους πατερες	τις μητερες	τα παιδια
toos pah-<u>teh</u>-res	*tis mee-<u>teh</u>-res*	*tah peh-dee-<u>ah</u>*
fathers	mothers	children

ADJECTIVES

Adjectives in Greek precede the noun but do not agree in ending.

Example: ο υψηλος πατερας, *oh ip-see-<u>los</u> pah-<u>teh</u>-ras*, the tall father (the father is tall) το παλιο σπιτι, *toh pah-lee-<u>oh</u> <u>spee</u>-tee*, the old house.

PERSONAL PRONOUNS

Nominative

I	εγω	*eh-<u>goh</u>*
you	εσυ	*es-<u>see</u>*
he, she, it	αυτος, αυτη, αυτο	*af-<u>tos</u>, af-<u>tee</u>, af-<u>toh</u>*
we	εμεις	*eh-<u>mees</u>*
you	εσεις	*es-<u>sees</u>*
they	αυτοι, αυτες, αυτα	*af-<u>tee</u>, af-<u>tes</u>, af-<u>tah</u>*

GRAMMAR 3

DIRECT OBJECT

Accusative

me	μου, εμενα	*moo, eh-<u>meh</u>-nah*
you	σου, εσενα	*soo, es-<u>seh</u>-nah*
him	του	*too*
her	της	*tees*
it	του	*too*
us	μας	*mahs*
you	σας	*sas*
they	τους	*toos*

POSSESSIVE ADJECTIVES

Possessive adjectives (my, your etc.) remain unchanged: the article which precedes them indicates the gender and the number:

Singular
masculine/feminine/neuter

my	ο / η / το ... μου	*o/i/toh ... moo*
your	ο / η / το ... σου	*o/i/toh ... soo*
his	ο / η / το ... του	*o/i/toh ... too*
our	ο / η / το ... μας	*o/i/toh ... mahs*
your	ο / η / το ... σας	*o/i/toh ... sahs*
their	ο / η / το ... τους	*o/i/toh ... toos*

Plural
masculine/feminine/neuter

my	οι / οι / τα ... μου	i/i/tah ... moo
your	οι / οι / τα ... σου	i/i/tah ... soo
his	οι / οι / τα ... του	i/i/tah ... too
our	οι / οι / τα ... μας	i/i/tah ... mahs
your	οι / οι / τα ... σας	i/i/tah ... sahs
their	οι / οι / τα ... τους	i/i/tah ... toos

Example:

ο αδελφος μου	oh ah-del-_fos_ moo	my brother
ο αδελφος σου	oh ah-del-_fos_ soo	your brother
ο αδελφος του	oh ah-del-_fos_ too	his brother
η αδελφη μου	ee ah-del-_fee_ moo	my sister
το παιδι μου	toh ped-_dee_ moo	my son

VERBS

Greek verbs are divided into two groups: in the first group, the last syllable (the ending) is stressed; in the other group, the stress falls on the last-but-one or second-to-last syllable. Note: Greek verbs are not listed as infinitives, as in English (to be, etc.) but under the first person singular, present indicative ("am").

Present

To live

ζω	*zoh*	I live
ζεις	*zees*	you live
ζει	*zee*	he lives
ζουμε	*zoo-meh*	we live
ζειτε	*zee-teh*	you live
ζουν	*zoon*	they live

To do

κανω	*kah-noh*	I do
κανεις	*kah-nis*	you do
κανει	*kah-nee*	he does
κανουμε	*kah-noo-meh*	we do
κανετε	*kah-neh-teh*	you do
κανουν	*kah-noon*	they do

Imperfect

εζουσα	*eh-zoos-sah*	I lived
εζουσες	*eh-zoos-sehs*	you lived
εζουσε	*eh-zoos-seh*	he lived
εζουσαμε	*eh-zoos-sah-meh*	we lived
εζουσαμε	*eh-zoos-ah-teh*	you lived
εζουσαν	*eh-zoos-ahn*	they lived

εκανα	*eh-kah-nah*	I did
εκανες	*eh-kah-nehs*	you did
εκανε	*eh-kah-neh*	he did
εκαναμε	*eh-kah-nah-meh*	we did
εκαναμε	*eh-kah-nah-teh*	you did
εκαναν	*eh-kah-nahn*	they did

Future

θα ζήσω	*thah-<u>zees</u>-soh*	I will live
θα ζήσεις	*thah-<u>zees</u>-sees*	you will live
θα ζήσει	*thah-<u>zees</u>-see*	he will lives
θα ζήσουμε	*thah-<u>zees</u>-soo-meh*	we will live
θα ζήσετε	*thah-<u>zees</u>-seh-teh*	you will live
θα ζήσουν	*thah-<u>zees</u>-soon*	they will live

θα κάνω	*thah-<u>kah</u>-noh*	I will do
θα κάνεις	*thah-<u>kah</u>-nees*	you will do
θα κάνει	*thah-<u>kah</u>-nee*	he will do
θα κάνουμε	*thah-<u>kah</u>-noo-meh*	we will do
θα κάνετε	*thah-<u>kah</u>-neh-teh*	you will do
θα κάνουν	*thah-<u>kah</u>-noon*	they will do

Present Perfect

εχω ζησει	<u>*eh*</u>-hoh <u>*zees*</u>-see	I have lived
εχεις ζησει	<u>*eh*</u>-his <u>*zees*</u>-see	you have lived
εχει ζησει	<u>*eh*</u>-hee <u>*zees*</u>-see	he has lived
εχουμε ζησει	<u>*eh*</u>-hoo-me <u>*zees*</u>-se	we have lived
εχετε ζησει	<u>*eh*</u>-heh-teh <u>*zees*</u>-see	you have lived
εχουν ζησει	<u>*eh*</u>-hoon <u>*zees*</u>-see	they have lived

εχω κανει	<u>*eh*</u>-ho <u>*kah*</u>-nee	I have done
εχεις κανει	<u>*eh*</u>-his <u>*kah*</u>-nee	you have done
εχει κανει	<u>*eh*</u>-hee <u>*kah*</u>-nee	he has done
εχουμε κανει	<u>*eh*</u>-hoo-meh <u>*kah*</u>-nee	we have done
εχετε κανει	<u>*eh*</u>-heh-teh <u>*kah*</u>-nee	you have done
εχουν κανει	<u>*eh*</u>-hoon <u>*kah*</u>-nee	they have done

GRAMMAR 7

Irregular verbs

To be

(εγω) ειμαι	*(eh-goh) ee*-meh	I am
(εσυ) εισαι	*(es-see) ees*-seh	you are
(αυτος) ειναι	*(af-tos) ee*-neh	he is
(εμεις) ειμαστε	*(eh-mees) ee*-mah-steh	we are
(εσεις) εισαστε	*(es-sees) ees*-ahs-teh	
(ειστε)	*(ees*-teh)	you are
(αυτοι) ειναι	*af-tee) ee*-neh	they are

To have

(εγω) εχω	*(eh-gch) eh*-hoh	I have
(εσυ) εχεις	*(es-see) eh*-his	you have
(αυτος) εχει	*(af-tos) eh*-hee	he has
(εμεις) εχουμε	*(eh-mees) eh*-hoo-meh	we have
(εσεις) εχετε	*(es-sis) eh*-heh-teh	you have
(αυτοι) εχουν	*(af-tee) eh*-hoon	they have

Can I have my bags taken up to my room?	Μπορειτε να μου φερετε επανω τη βαλιτσα μου; *boh-<u>ree</u>-teh nah moo <u>feh</u>-reh-teh eh-<u>pah</u>-noh tee vah-<u>leet</u>-tsah moo?*
At what time is breakfast/ lunch/ supper served?	Τι ωρα σερβιρετε το πρωινο/ το γευμα το βραδυνο; *tee <u>oh</u>-rah ser-<u>vee</u>-reh-teh toh proh-ee-<u>noh</u>/toh <u>yev</u>-mah/toh vrah-dee-<u>noh</u>?*
Can we have breakfast in our room at … ?	Μπορουμε να εχουμε το πρωινο στο δωματιο στις...; *boh-<u>roo</u>-meh nah <u>eh</u>-hoo-meh toh proh-ee-<u>noh</u> stoh doh-<u>mah</u>-tee-oh stis …?*
Can I have my key?	Μπορω να εχω το κλειδι μου; *boh-<u>roh</u> nah <u>eh</u>-hoh toh klee-<u>dee</u> moo?*
Put it on my bill	Βαλτε το στο λογαριασμο μου *<u>vahl</u>-teh toh stoh loh-gah-ree-ahs-<u>moh</u> moo*
I'd like an outside line, please	Μου δινετε γραμμη, σας παρακαλω; *moo <u>dee</u>-neh-teh grahm-<u>mee</u>, sahs pah-rah-kah-<u>loh</u>?*
May I have another blanket / another pillow?	Μπορω να εχω ακομη μια κουβερτα / ενα μαξιλαρι; *boh-<u>roh</u> nah <u>eh</u>-hoh ah-<u>kom</u>-mee mee-ah koo-<u>ver</u>-tah/<u>eh</u>-na mahx-see-<u>lah</u>-ree*
I have locked myself out of my room	Εμεινα εξω απο το δωματιο μου με το κλειδι στη πορτα *<u>eh</u>-mee-nah <u>eks</u>-soh ah-<u>poh</u> toh doh-<u>mah</u>-tee-oh moo meh toh klee-<u>thee</u> stee <u>por</u>-tah*

I'd like to book a single/ double room	Θα ηθελα να κλεισω ενα μονο δωματιο/ διπλο *thah ee-theh-lah nah klis-soh eh-nah moh-noh doh-mah-tee-oh/ dip-loh*
I'd like a room with breakfast/half board/full board	Θα ηθελα ενα δωματιο με το πρωινο/ μιση πανσιον/ πανσιον κομπλε *thah ee-theh-lah eh-nah doh-mah tee-oh meh toh proh-ee-noh/ miss-see pahn-see-ohn/pahn-see ohn kom-pleh*
How much does it cost per day/ per week?	Ποσο κοστιζει την ημερα/ την εβδομαδα; *pos-soh kos-tee-zee tin ee-meh-rah/tin ev-doh-mah-dah?*
Is breakfast included in the price?	Το πρωινο ειναι μεσα στη τιμη; *toh proh-ee-noh ee-neh mes-sah stee tee-mee?*
We will be stopping for three nights from… till …	Θα μεινουμε τρις νυκτες απο τις… μεχρι τις… *thah mee-noo-meh tris nik-tes ah-poh tis … meh-ree tis …*
We will arrive at …	Θα φθασουμε στις… *that ftahs-soo-meh stis …*
We have booked a room in the name of …	Κλεισαμε ενα δωματιο στο ονομα… *klis-sah-meh eh-nah doh-mah-tee-oh stoh oh-noh-mah …*

Things to remember

> Greek currency has bank notees in denominations of
> 10,000, 5,000, 1,000, 500 and 100 drachmas; the coins
> are of 100, 50, 20, 10, 5 and 1 drachma. As a result of
> the ever-increasing inflation, the drachma as a single coin
> no longer has much value.

I don't have enough money	Δεν εχω αρκετα χρηματα *den eh-hoh ar-keh-tah hree-mah-tah*
Do you have any change?	Εχετε να μου αλλαξετε; *eh-heh-teh nah moo ah-lahks-eh-teh?*
Can you change a 10,000-drachma note for me?	Μπορειτε να μου αλλαξετε 10000 δραχμες; *boh-ree-teh nah moo ah-lahks-eh-teh deh-kah hee-lee-ah-des drah-mes?*
I would like to change these pounds/dollars to drachmas	Θελω να αλλαξω αγγλικες λιρες/δολλαρια σε δραχμες *theh-loh nah ah-lahk-soh tis ah-glee-kehs lee-rehs/thoh-lah-ree-ah seh drah-mes*
What is the exchange rate for the pound/dollar	Ποια ειναι η τιμη του συνναλαγματος για αγγλικη λιρα/δολλαριο *pee-ah ee-neh ee tee-mee too see-nah-lahg-mah-tos yah ah-glee-kehs lee-rehs thoh-lah-ree-ah*

NUMBERS

0 μηδεν *mee-<u>den</u>*	17 δεκαεπτα *deh-kah-ep-<u>tah</u>*	200 διακοσια *dee-ah-<u>kos</u>-see-ah*
1 ενα *<u>eh</u>-nah*	18 δεκαοκτω *deh-kah-ok-<u>toh</u>*	300 τριακοσια *tree-ah-<u>kos</u>-see-ah*
2 δυο *<u>dee</u>-oh*	19 δεκαεννεα *deh-kah-en-<u>neh</u>-ah*	1000 χιλια *<u>hee</u>-lee-ah*
3 τρια *<u>tree</u>-ah*	20 εικοσι *ee-<u>kos</u>-see*	2000 δυο χιλιαδες *<u>dee</u>-oh hee-lee-<u>ah</u>-des*
4 τεσσερα *<u>tes</u>-seh-rah*	21 εικοσιενα *ee-kos-see-<u>eh</u>-nah*	1000000
5 πεντε *<u>pen</u>-deh*	22 εικοσιδυο *ee-kos-see-<u>dee</u>-oh*	ενα εκατομμυριο *<u>eh</u>-nah eh-kah-toh-<u>mee</u>-ree-oh*
6 εξι *<u>eks</u>-ee*	23 εικοσιτρια *ee-kos-see-<u>tree</u>-ah*	
7 επτα *ep-<u>tah</u>*	30 τριαντα *tree-<u>ahn</u>-dah*	1st πρωτος *<u>proh</u>-tos*
8 οκτω *ok-<u>toh</u>*	40 σαραντα *sah-<u>rahn</u>-dah*	2nd δευτερος *<u>def</u>-teh-ros*
9 εννεα *en-<u>neh</u>-ah*	50 πενηντα *peh-<u>neen</u>-dah*	3rd τριτος *<u>tree</u>-tos*
10 δεκα *<u>deh</u>-kah*	60 εξηντα *eks-<u>seen</u>-dah*	4th τεταρτος *<u>teh</u>-tar-tos*
11 εντεκα *<u>en</u>-deh-kah*	70 εβδομηντα *ev-doh-<u>meen</u>-dah*	5th πεμπτος *<u>pem</u>-ptos*
12 δωδεκα *<u>doh</u>-deh-kah*	80 ογδοντα *og-<u>don</u>-dah*	6th εκτος *<u>ek</u>-tos*
13 δεκατρια *deh-kah-<u>tree</u>-ah*	90 εννενηντα *enn-nen-<u>neen</u>-dah*	7th εβδομος *<u>ev</u>-doh-mos*
14 δεκατεσσερα *deh-kah-<u>tes</u>-seh-rah*	100 εκατο *eh-kah-<u>toh</u>*	8th ογδωος *<u>og</u>-doh-os*
15 δεκαπεντε *deh-kah-<u>pen</u>-deh*	101 εκατονενα *eh-kah-toh-<u>neh</u>-nah*	9th ενατος *<u>eh</u>-nah-tos*
16 δεκαεξι *deh-kah-<u>eks</u>-ee*	110 εκατονδεκα *eh-kah-ton-<u>deh</u>-kah*	10th δεκατος *<u>deh</u>-kah-tos*

What are these/those?	Τι ειναι αυτα/ εκεινα *Tee ee-neh ahf-tah/ eh-kee-nah?*
What's in this cake?	Τι εχει μεσα αυτη η τουρτα; *tee eh-hee mes-sah ahf-tee ee toor-tah?*
I would like a small/medium size tray of pastries	Θα ηθελα ενα μικρο δισκακι/ μετριο με παστες *thah ee-theh-lah ee-nah mee-kroh dis-kah-kee/meh-tree-oh meh pahs-tes*
I would like an assortment of pastries.	Θα ηθελα ποικιλια απο παστες *thah ee-theh-lah pee-kee-lee-ah ah-poh pas-tes*
I'll have a cone for 200 drachmas with vanilla and chocolate, with/without whipped cream	Θελω ενα κονο των 200 δραχμων με κρεμα και σοκολατα, με σαντιγυ/ διχως σαντιγυ *theh-loh ee-nah koh-noh ton dee-ah-kos-see-on drah-mon meh kreh-mah keh soh-koh-lah-tah, meh san-tee-yee/dee-hos san-tee-yee*
How much does it/do they cost?	Ποσο κοστιζει/ κοστιζουν; *pos-soh kos-tee-zee/kos-tee-zoon?*
Is there chocolate in those cakes?	Εχουν σοκολατα αυτες οι παστες; *eh-hoon soh-koh-lah-tah ahf-tes ee pahs-tes?*

How much is it?	Ποσο κοστιζει; *pohs-soh kos-tee-zee?*
Can I have the bill, please?	Μου φερνετε τον λογαριασμο, παρακαλω; *moo fer-neh-teh ton loh-gah-ree-ahs-moh, pah-rah-kah-loh?*
May I pay by credit card?	Μπορω να πληρωσω με καρτα πιστεως; *boh-roh nah plee-ros-soh meh kahr-tah pees-teh-os?*
Do you accept checks/ traveler's checks?	Δεχεσθε επιταγες/ τραβελερς τσεκ; *deh-hes-teh eh-pee-tah-yes/ traveler's checks?*
May I have the receipt, please?	Μου δινετε την αποδειξη, σας παρακαλω; *moo dee-neh-teh teehn ah-poh-dix-ee, sahs pah-rah-kah-loh?*
Is the service / VAT included?	Το σερβιρισμα ειναι μεσα στη τιμη/το Α.Φ.Μ; *toh ser-vee-ris-mah ee-neh meh-sah sti tee-mee/ toh A.Fi.Mi.?*
What does that come to?	Ποσο ειναι συνολικως; *pos-soh ee-neh see-noh-lee-kos?*
Do I have to leave a deposit ?	Πρεπει να σας αφησω μια προκαταβολη; *preh-pee nah sahs ah-fees-soh mee-ah pro-kah-tah-voh-lee*
I think you have given me the wrong change	Μου φαινεται πως μου δωσατε λαθος ρεστα *moo feh-neh-teh pos moo dos-sah-teh lah-thos res-tah*

Can you help me, please?	Μπορειτε να με βοηθησετε, σας παρακαλω; *boh-ree-teh nah meh voy-thees-seh-teh, sahs pah-rah-kah-loh?*
What is the matter?	Τι συμβαινει; *tee sim-veh-nee?*
What's going on?	Τι τρεχει; *tee treh-hee?*
I need some help	Εχω αναγκη απο βοηθεια *eh-ho ah-nah-gee ah-poh voh-ee-thee-ah*
I don't understand	Δεν καταλαβαινω1 *den kah-tah-lah-veh-noh*
Do you speak English?	Μιλατε αγγλικα; *mee-lah-teh ah-glee-kah?*
Can you repeat that, please?	Μπορειτε να επαναλαβετε, παρακαλω; *boh-ree-teh nah eh-pah-nah-lah-veh-teh, pah-rah-kah-loh?*
I've run out of money	Εμεινα διχως χρηματα *eh-mee-nah dee-hos hree-mah-tah*
I can't find my son/ my daughter	Δεν βρισκω πια την κορη μου/ το γυιο μου *den vrees-koh pee-ah tin koh-ree moo / toh yee-oh moo*
I've lost my way	Εχω χαθει *eh-hoh hah-thee*
Leave me alone!	Μ'αφηνετε ησυχο! *mah-fee-neh-teh ees-see-hoh!*

PRONUNCIATION 1

Our biggest problem in reading Greek is that the alphabet's script is different. However, most of the sounds are identical to those of our alphabet. It really does not require much time to learn the basics of this language.

To overcome the first moments of difficulty, read the italicized phrase under the Greek sentence specially designed for English speakers. The italics provide the pronunciation of Greek as it would appear in our own alphabet. The stressed syllable is underlined.

Greek script	*English pronunciation*	*Phonetic transcription*
A α	as our short **a** in «almond»	*ah*
B β	as our **v**	*v*
Γ γ	as the **g** in «gander»; or when followed by ε or ια it is pronounced as the **y** in «yellow»	*g* *y*
Δ δ	as our **th** in «the»	*dee*
E ε	as **e** as in «step»	*eh*
Z ζ	as the **s** in «rose»	*z*
H η	as **ee** in «steep»	*ee*
Θ θ	as **th** as in «theater»	*th*
I ι	as **ee** in «steep»	*ee*
K κ	as **k** in «kite»	*k*
Λ λ	is our **l**	*l*
M μ	is our **m**	*m*
N ν	is our **n**	*n*
Ξ ξ	pronounced as an **x**	*x*
O o	is our **o**	*oh*
Π π	is our **p**	*p*
P ρ	is our **r**	*r*
Σ σ, ς	is our **s** as in «six»	*s*

T	τ	as our **t**;	
		preceded by ζ	*t*
		it sounds like **dg**	*d*
Y	υ	pronounced as **ee** in «steep»	*ee*
Φ	φ	as our **f**	*f*
X	χ	as **h** in «house»	*h*
Ψ	ψ	pronounced as **ps**	*ps*
Ω	ω	as long **o** in «old»	*oh*

Consonant groups

γκ	as a hard **g**; the k is mute	*g*
μπ	pronounced as **b** (at times **mb**)	*b (mb)*
ντ	the **t** is pronounced as **d**	*nd*
τσ	as the **z** in «Ritz»	*ts*
τζ	as **ds** in Leeds	*z*

Diphthongs

αι	is short **e** as in «step»	*eh*
αϊ	is read as «eye»	*ah-ee*
αυ	is read as **af** or **av**	*af, av*
ει	is read as **ee**	*ee*
ευ	is read as **ef** or **ev**	*ef, av*
οι	is read as **ee**	*ee*
ου	is read as **oo** as in «good»	*oo*
υι	is read as **ee**	*ee*

New Year's Day	Πρωτοχρονια *proh-toh-hroh-nee-<u>ah</u>*
Epiphany (6 January)	Επιφανεια *eh-pee-<u>fah</u>-nee-ah*
8 January Woman's Day (matriarchal feast)	8 Ιανουαριου (γυναικοκρατια) *ok-<u>toh</u> ee-ah-noo-ah-<u>ree</u>-oo* *(yee-neh-koh-krah-<u>tee</u>-ah)*
Carnival	Καρναβαλι *kar-nah-<u>vah</u>-lee*
Good Friday	Μεγαλη Παρασκευη *meh-<u>gah</u>-lee pah-rahs-keh-<u>vee</u>*
Easter	Πασχα *<u>pahs</u>-hah*
25 March (National Holiday)	25 Μαρτιου *ee-koh-see-<u>pen</u>-teh mahr-<u>tee</u>-oo*
1st May	1 Μαιου *<u>proh</u>-tee mah-<u>ee</u>-oo*
Naval Week (end June/July)	Ναυτικη εβδομαδα *nahf-tee-<u>kee</u> ev-doh-<u>mah</u>-dah*
Wine Feast	Γιορτη του κρασιου *yee-or-<u>tee</u> too krahs-see-<u>oo</u>*
Assumption Day	Δεκαπενταυγουστος *deh-kah-pen-<u>tav</u>-goos-tohs*
28 October (National Holiday)	28 Οκτωβριου *ee-kos-tee-og-<u>doh</u>-ee ok-tohv-<u>ree</u>-oo*
Christmas	Χριστουγεννα *Hris-<u>too</u>-yee-eh-nah*

Where is the restroom please?	Που ειναι η τουαλετα, σας παρακαλω; *poo <u>ee</u>-neh ee twah-lehtah, sas pah-rah-kah-<u>loh</u>?*
Do you have to pay for the restrooms?	Η τουαλετα ειναι με πληρωμη; *ee twah-lehtaht <u>ee</u>-neh meh plee-roh-<u>mee</u>?*
There's no toilet paper/ soap	Δεν εχει χαρτι τουαλετας/ σαπουνι *den <u>eh</u>-hee har-<u>tee</u> twah-<u>let</u>-tas/ sah-<u>poo</u>-nee*
Is there a restroom for the disabled?	Υπαρχει τουαλετα για αναπηρους; *ee-<u>pahr</u>-hee twah-lehtah yah ah-nah-<u>pee</u>-roos?*
The toilet is blocked/jammed	Το μπανιο ειναι βουλομενο *toh <u>bah</u>-nee-oh <u>ee</u>-neh voo-loh-<u>meh</u>-noh*

SMOKING

Things to remember

Although there is no law against smoking in public places in Greece, when one comes across a sign "απαγορευεται το καπνισμα", one should not light a cigarette, a cigar, or a pipe.

Can I smoke here?	Επιτρεπεται εδω το καπνισμα; *eh-pee-<u>treh</u>-peh-teh eh-<u>doh</u> toh <u>kap</u>-niz-mah?*
Do you mind if I smoke?	Σας πειραζει, αν καπνισω; *sahs pee-<u>rah</u>-zee, ahn kap-<u>nees</u>-soh?*
May I have an ash-tray?	Μπορω να εχω ενα τασακι; *boh-<u>roh</u> nah eh-hoh eh-na tas-<u>sah</u>-kee?*
Do you have any matches?	Εχετε σπιρτα; *<u>eh</u>-heh-teh <u>speer</u>-tah?*
Do you have a light?	Εχετε να αναψετε; *<u>eh</u>-heh-teh nah ah-<u>nahp</u>-seh-teh?*
Do you mind putting out that cigarette?	Σας πειραζει να μην καπνιζετε; *sahs pee-<u>rah</u>-zee nah min kahp-<u>neez</u>-zeh-teh?*

Could you call me a taxi, please?	Μπορειτε να μου καλεσετε ενα ταξι παρακαλω; *boh-ree-teh nah moo kah-les-seh-teh eh-nah tak-see pah-rah-kah-loh?*
To the airport/To the main train station	Στο αεροδρομιο/ στο σταθμο των τραινων *stoh ah-ehr-oh-droh-mee-oh/stoh stath-moh ton treh-non*
Take me to this address/this hotel	Να με πατε σ'αυτυ τη διευθυνση/ σ'αυτο το ξενοδοχειο *nah meh pah-teh sahf-tee tee dee-ehf-thin-see/ sahf-toh toh kseh-noh-doh-hee-oh*
Is it far?	Ειναι μακρια; *ee-neh mah-kree-ah?*
I'm in a hurry	Ειμαι πολυ βιαστικος *ee-meh poh-lee vee-ahs-tee-kos*
How much will it cost?	Ποσο θα κοστισει; *pos-soh thah kos-tees-see?*
Stop here/at the corner	Σταματηστε εδω/ στη γωνια *stah-mah-tees-teh eh-doh/stee goh-nee-ah*
How much is it?	Ποσο ειναι; *pos-soh ee-neh?*
Can I have a receipt?	Μπορειτε να μου δωσετε αποδειξη; *boh-ree-teh nah moo dos-seh-teh ah-poh-dik-see?*
Keep the change	Κρατηστε τα ρεστα *krah-tees-teh tah res-tah*

Things to remember

In order to use public telephones, it is necessary to buy a tee-leh-<u>kahr</u>-tah, issued by the H.T.O. (Hellenic Telecommunications Organisation) and which are usually sold at newsstands or the postoffice. They come in telecards of 1,000 or 2,000 drachmas. If you do not have a card with you, or if for any reason you cannot obtain one, you can go directly to the nearest H.T.O. office or to any public place (hotel or restaurant) and call through the operator.

Is there a phone?	Υπαρχει ενα τηλεφωνο; ee-<u>pahr</u>-hee eh-nah tee-leh-foh-noh?
Can you give me a "tilecarta" of 1,000/ 2,000 drachmas?	Μου δινετε μια τηλεκαρτα των 1000/ 2000 δραχμων; moo <u>dee</u>-neh-teh <u>mee</u>-ah tee-leh-<u>kar</u>-tah ton hee-<u>lee</u>-on/<u>dee</u>-oh hee-lee-<u>ah</u>-don drah-<u>mon</u>?
I'd like to make a call	Θα ηθελα να κανω ενα τηλεφωνημα thah <u>ee</u>-theh-lah nah <u>kah</u>-noh eh-nah tee-leh-<u>foh</u>-nee-mah
The number is … extension …	Ο αριθμος ειναι... oh ah-rith-<u>mohs</u> ee-neh ..., ess-oh-teh-ree-<u>koh</u> …
How much is it to phone the United States/Great Britain?	Ποσο κοστιζει το τυλεφωνημα για τις Ηνωμενες Πολιτειες/ Αγγλια <u>pohs</u>-soh kos-<u>stee</u>-tsee toh tee-leh-<u>foh</u>-nee-mah yah tis Ee-noh-<u>meh</u>-nes Po-lee-<u>tee</u>-es/Ag-<u>lee</u>-ah
What is the prefix for … ?	Ποιος ειναι ο κωδικος για... pee-<u>ohs</u> ee-neh oh koh-dee-<u>kos</u> yah …

The line's busy	Η γραμμη ειναι πιασμενη *ee grahm-mee ee-neh pee-ahs-meh-nee*
Hello, this is …	Εμπρος, ειμαι ο... *em-bros ee-meh oh …*
Can I speak to…?	Μπορω να μιλησω με...; *boh-roh nah mee-lees-soh meh … ?*
I've been cut off	Μου εκοπηκε η επικοινωνια *moo eh-koh-pee-keh ee eh-pee-kee-noh-nee-yah*
I'm sorry, wrong number	Συγνωμη, εκανα λαθος στον αριθμο *sig-noh-mee, eh-kah-nah lah-thos ston ah-rith-moh*
I can't hear you very well	Δεν ακουγεται καλα *den ah-koo-yeh-teh kah-lah*

YOU MAY HEAR:

Ναι, ποιος ειναι; *neh, pee-os ee-neh?*	Yes, who is it?
Περιμενετε στο ακουστικο σας *peh-ree-meh-neh-teh stoh ah-koos-tee-koh sahs*	Hold the line
Ξαναπαρτε αργοτερα, σας παρακαλω *ksah-nah-par-teh ar-goh-teh-rah, sahs pah-rah-kah-loh*	Could you call back later, please
Δεν ειναι εδω/ λειπει *den ee-neh eh-doh/lee-pee*	He is not at home/ He's not in
Κανατε λαθος αριθμο *kah-nah-teh lah-thos ah-rith-moh*	You've got the wrong number

What time is it?	Τι ωρα ειναι; *tee <u>oh</u>-rah <u>ee</u>-neh?*
It's …	Ειναι... η ωρα *<u>ee</u>-neh ee <u>oh</u>-rah*
8.00	Οκτω *ok-<u>toh</u>*
8.05	Οκτω και πεντε *ok-<u>toh</u> keh <u>pen</u>-deh*
8.10	Οκτω και δεκα *ok-<u>toh</u> keh <u>deh</u>-kah*
8.15	Οκτω και δεκαπεντε/οκτω και τεταρτο *ok-<u>toh</u> keh deh-kah-<u>pen</u>-deh/keh <u>teh</u>-tar-toh*
8.20	Οκτω και εικοσι *ok-<u>toh</u> keh <u>ee</u>-kos-see*
8.30	Οκτω και τριαντα/ εννεα οκτω και μιση *ok-<u>toh</u> keh tree-<u>ahn</u>-dah/ok-<u>toh</u> keh mis-<u>see</u>*
8.40	Οκτω και σαραντα/ εννεα παρα εικοσι *ok-<u>toh</u> keh sah-<u>ran</u>-dah/eh-<u>neh</u>-ah pah-<u>rah</u> <u>ee</u>-kos-see*
8.45	Οκτω και σαρανταπεντε/ εννεα παρα τεταρτο *ok-<u>toh</u> keh sah-ran-dah-<u>pen</u>-deh/eh-<u>neh</u>-ah pah-<u>rah</u> <u>teh</u>-tar-toh*
8.50	Οκτω και πενηντα/ εννεα παρα δεκα *ok-<u>toh</u> keh pen-<u>neen</u>-dah/en-<u>neh</u>-ah pah-<u>rah</u> <u>deh</u>-kah*

8.00 A.M. / P.M.	Οκτω το πρωι/ το βραδυ *Ok-toh toh pro-ee/ toh vrah-dee*
Noon	Μεσημερι *mes-see-meh-ree*
Midnight	Μεσανυχτα *mes-sah-nih-tah*
What time do you open?/ close?	Τι ωρα ανοιγετε/ κλεινετε; *tee oh-rah ah-nee-yeh-teh/klee-neh-teh?*
What time does the restaurant close?	Τι ωρα κλεινει το ρεστωραντ; *tee oh-rah klee-nee toh rehs-toh-rahnt?*
At what time do the stores close?	Τι ωρα κλεινουν τα μαγαζια; *tee oh-rah klee-noon tah mah-gah-zee-ah?*
How long will it take us to get there?	Ποση ωρα χρειαζεται για να φθασω; *pohs-see oh-rah hree-ah-zeh-teh yah nah fthas-soh?*
We arrived early/late	Φθασαμε νωρις/ αργα *fthas-sah-meh noh-rees/ar-gah*
It's early/late	Ειναι νωρις/ αργα *ee-neh noh-rees/ar-gah*
What time does the bus leave?	Τι ωρα φευγει το λεωφορειο; *tee or-rah fev-gee toh leh-oh-foh-ree-oh?*
The table is booked for ... this evening	Το τραπεζι ειναι κλεισμενο για τις... αποψε *toh trah-peh-zee ee-neh klis-meh-noh yah tis ... ah-pop-seh*

UNITS OF MEASURE

A half liter of …	Μισο λιτρο … *mis-soh lee-troh …*
A liter of ..	Ενα λιτρο… *eh-na lee-troh …*
A kilo of …	Ενα κιλο… *eh-na kee-loh …*
Half a kilo of …	Μισο κιλο… *mis-soh kee-loh …*
A hundred grams of …	Εκατο γραμμαρια… *eh-kah-toh gram-mah-ree-ah …*
A slice of …	Ενα κοματι… *eh-nah koh-mah-tee …*
A portion of …	Μια μεριδα… *mee-ah meh-ree-dah …*
A dozen of …	Μια δωδεκαδα… *mee-ah doh-deh-kah-dah …*
Two thousand drachmas of …	δυο χιλιαδες δραχμες… *dee-oh hee-lee-ah-des drah-mes ….*

GASTRONOMIC
DICTIONARY

acid ξυνο *ksee-noh*
action πραξη *prah-ksee*
address διευθυνση *dee-ef-thin-see*
adult ενηλικος *eh-nee-lee-kos*
age ηλικια *ee-lee-kee-ah*
ahead εμπρος *em-bros*
air αερας *ah-eh-rahs*
airconditioned κλιματισμος *klee-mah-tis-mos*
airplane αεροπλανο *ah-eh-roh-plah-noh*
airport αεροδρομιο *ah-eh-roh-droh-mee-oh*
all ολο *oh-loh* το παν *toh pahn*
allergy αλεργια *ah-ler-gee-ah*
almonds αμυγδαλα *ah-mig-dah-lah*
always παντοτε *pahn-doh-teh*
American (man) Αμερικανός *ah-meh-ree-kah-nos*
American (woman) Αμερικανιδα *ah-meh-ree-kah-nee-dah*
anchovy ατζουγια *ah-zoo-yah*
aniseed γλυκανισο *glee-kahn-ee-soh*
antibiotic αντιβιοτικο *ahn-dee-vee-oh-tee-koh*
any οτιδηποτε *oh-tee-dee-poh-teh*

aperitif ορεκτικο ποτο *oh-rehk-tee-koh poh toh*
appetite ορεξη *oh-rek-see*
apple μηλο *mee-loh*
appointment ραντεβου *rahn-deh-voo*
approach, to πλησιαζω *plis-see-ah-zoh*
apricot βερυκοκο *veh-ree-koh-koh*
April Απριλιος *ah-pree-lee-os*
Arab Αραβας *ah-rah-vas*
aroma αρωμα *ah-roh-ma*
aromatic αρωματικος *ah-roh-mah-tee-kos*
aromatic herbs αρωματικα φυτα *ah-roh-mah-tee-kah fee-tah*
arrive, to φθανω *ftah-no*
artichoke αγκιναρα *ah-gee-nah-rah*
ashtray τασακι *tahs-sah-kee*
ask, to ερωτω *eh-roh-toh*
asparagus σπαραγγια *spah-rah-gee-ah*
aspirin ασπιρινη *ahs-pee-ree-nee*
at once αμεσως *ah-mess-sohs*
Athens Αθηνα *ah-thee-nah*
Attica Αττικη *ah-tee-kee*
August Αυγουστος *ahv-goos-tos*

authentic αυθεντικο *ahf-teh-tee-koh*
avocado αβοκαδο *ah-voh-kah-doh*
avoid, to αποφευγω *ah-poh-fev-goh*

backwards πισω *pis-soh*
bad κακως *kah-kos*
banana μπανανα *bah-nah-nah*
bank τραπεζα *trah-peh-zah*
banknote χαρτονομισμα *har-toh-noh-mis-mah*
bar μπαρ *bar*
barley κριθαρι *kree-thah-ree*
basil βασιλικος *vahs-see-lee-kos*
bass τσιπουρα *tsee-poo-rah*
bath μπανιο *bah-nee-oh*
bay δαφνη *dahf-nee*
be, to ειμαι *ee-meh*
beans φασολια *fah-soh-lee-ah*
beautiful ωραιος *oh-reh-os*
bechamel μπεσαμελα *bess-sah-meh-lah*
beef βοδι *voh-dee*
beer μπυρα *bee-rah*
beetroot πατζαρι *pah-zah-ree*
beginning εναρξη *eh-nar-ksee* αρχη *ahr-hee*
behind πισω *peess-soh*

bell pepper πιπερια *pee-peh-ree-ah*
better καλυτερα *kah-lee-teh-rah*
between σε *seh*
beverage αναψυκτικο *ah-nahp-sik-tee-koh*
big, great μεγαλος *meh-gah-los,* πελωριο *peh-loh-ree-oh*
bill λογαριασμος *loh-gah-ree-ahs-mos*
biscuit κουλουρακι *koo-loo-rah–kee*
bitter πικρο *pik-roh*
black μαυρο *mahv-roh*
blood αιμα *eh-mah*
Boetia Βοιωτια *vee-oh-tee-ah*
boil, to βραζω *vrah-zoh*
boiled βραστο *vrah-stoh*
boiling ζεματιστο *tseh-mah-tis-toh*
bone κοκαλο *koh-kah-loh*
book βιβλιο *viv-lee-oh*
bottargo ταραμας *tah-rah-mahs*
bottle μπουκαλι *boo-khah-lee*
bottle-opener τιρμπουσον *tir-boo-son*
bottled εμφυαλωμενο *em-fee-ah-loh-meh-noh*
bovine μοσχαρι *mohs-hah-ree*

brains μυαλο *mee-ah-<u>loh</u>*
braised της κατσαρολας *tis kah-tsah-<u>roh</u>-las*
bread ψωμι *psoh-<u>mee</u>*
breakfast πρωινο γευμα *proh-ee-<u>noh</u> yev-mah*
breast στηθος *stee-thos*
bring, to φερνω *<u>fehr</u>-noh*
broad beans κουκια *koo-kee-<u>ah</u>*
broccoli κραμβη *<u>khram</u>-vee*
broth ζωμος *zoh-<u>mos</u>*
burned καμμενο *kahm-<u>meh</u>-noh*
bus λεωφορειο *leh-oh-foh-<u>ree</u>-oh*
but αλλα *ahl-<u>lah</u>*
butcher's χασαπικο *has-<u>sah</u>-pee-koh*
butter βουτυρο *<u>voo</u>-tee-roh*
button κουμπι *koo-<u>bee</u>*
buy, to αγοραζω *ah-goh-<u>rah</u>-zoh*

cabbage λαχανο *<u>lah</u>-hah-noh*
cabernet καμπερνε *kah-ber-<u>neh</u>*
calm ηρεμος *ee-reh-mos*
calories θερμιδες *ther-<u>mee</u>-des*
camomile χαμομηλι *hah-moh-<u>mee</u>-lee*
cancel to ακυρωνω *ah-kee-<u>roh</u>-noh*

cancel, to διαγραφω *dee-ah-<u>grah</u>-foh*
candied καντυ *<u>kahn</u>-dee*
candle κερι *keh-<u>ree</u>*
cannelloni κανελονια *kah-neh-<u>loh</u>-nee-ah*
capers καπαρη *<u>kah</u>-pah-ree*
cardoons γαιδουραγκαθο *gah-ee-doo-<u>rah</u>-ghah-thoh*
careful προσοχη *proh-soh-<u>hee</u>*
careful, to be προσεξτε *proh-<u>seks</u>-teh*
cashier ταμειας *tah-<u>mee</u>-ahs*
cassata ice-cream κασατο παγωτο *kahs-<u>sah</u>-toh pah-goh-<u>toh</u>*
casserole κατσαρολα *kaht-sah-<u>roh</u>-lah*
cauliflower κουνουπιδι *koo-noo-<u>pee</u>-dee*
celery σελινο *<u>seh</u>-lee-noh*
cellar καβα *<u>kah</u>-vah*
cereals δημητριακα *dee-mee-tree-ah-<u>kah</u>*
change συναλλαγμα *see-nah-lahg-mah*
change, to αλλαζω *ah-<u>lahzoh</u>*
charge, to χρεωνω *hreh-<u>oh</u>-noh*
check (cheque) επιταγη *eh-pee-tah-<u>yee</u>*
checkout (cashier's) ταμειον *tah-<u>mee</u>-on*

cheese τυρι *tee-ree*
cherry (black) βυσσινο *vis-see-noh*
cherry κερασι *keh-rahs-see*
chestnut καστανο *kahs-tah-noh*
chew, to μασω *mahs-soh*
chicken κοτοπουλο *koh-toh-poo-loh*
chickpeas ρεβυθια *reh-vee-thee-ah*
chicory ραδικια *rah-dee-kyah*
child παιδακι *peh-dah-kee*
chili pepper πιπερια καυτερη *pee-peh-ree-ah kahf-teh-ree*
chop χοιρινη μπριζολα *hee-ree-nee bri-zoh-lah*
Christmas Χριστουγεννα *hris-too-ghen-nah*
cigarette τσιγαρο *tsee-gah-roh*
cinnamon κανελα *kah-neh-lah*
citrus (fruits) εσπεριδοειδη *es-per-ee-doh-ee-dee*
city πολις *poh-lis*
clams αχιβαδες *ah-hee-vah-des*
clean καθαρο *kah-thah-roh*
close, to κλεινω *klee-noh*
cloves γαρυφαλα *gah-ree-fah-lah*
cocoa κακαο *kah-kah-oh*

coconut καρυδα *kah-ree-dah*
cod μπακαλιαρος *bah-kah-lee-ah-ros*
cod, fried μπακαλιαρος τηγανητος *bah-kah-lee-ah-ros tee-gah nee-tos*
codfish fillet μπακαλιαρακια *bah-kah-lee-ah-rah-kee-ah*
coffee καφες *kah-fes*
cold κρυο *kree-oh*
come, to ερχομαι *ehr-hoh-meh*
company (business) επιχειρηση *eh-pee-hee-ris-see*
complaint παραπονα *pah-rah-poh-nah*
condiment καρυκευμα *kah-ree-kev-mah*
contact lens φακοι επαφης *fah-kee eh-pah-fis*
corner γωνια *goh-nee-ah*
country χωρα *hoh-rah* χωριο *hoh-ree-oh*
country εξοχη *eks-oh-hee*
countrystyle χωριατικη *hoh-ree-ah-tee-kee*
cover charge κουβερ *koo-ver* σκεπαστο *skeh-pahs-toh*
crab καβουρας *kah-voo-ras*
crayfish γαριδες *gah-ree-des*
cream σαντιγυ *sahn-tee-yee*

creampuff λουκουμασ *loo-koo-mahs*
credit card καρτα πιστεως *kar-tah pis-teh-os*
Crete Κρητη *kree-tee*
cucumber αγγουρι *ah-goo-ree*
cup φλυτζανι *flee-tzah-nee*
cut, to κοβω *koh-voh*
cutlery μαχαιροπιρουνα *mah-heh-roh-pee-roo-nah*
Cyclades Κυκλαδες *kik-lah-des*
Cyprus Κυπρος *kee-prohs*

daily εφημεριδα *eh-fee-meh-ree-dah*
dance, to χορευω *hoh-reh-voh*
dates (fruit) χουρμαδες *hoor-mah-des*
daughter κορη *koh-ree*
day ημερα *ee-meh-rah*
December Δεκεμβριος *deh-kem-vree-ohs*
Demestica Δεμεστιχα *deh-mes-tee-hah*
diabetic διαβητικος *dee-ah-vee-tee-kos*
diet διαιτα *dee-eh-tah*
difficult δυσκολος *dees-koh-los*
digestible ευπεπτο *ef-pep-toh*
digestive χωνευτικο *hoh-nef-tee-koh*

directions κατευθυνση *kah-tef-thin-see*
director, manager διευθυντης *dee-eft-hin-dees*
dirty βρωμικος *vroh-mee-kos*
disabled αναπηρος *ah-nah-pee-ros*
discothèque δισκοθηκη *dis-koh-thee-kee*
distance αποσταση *ah-pos-tahs-see*
disturb, to ενοχλω *eh-noh-loh*
doctor γιατρος *yee-ah-tros*
documents χαρτια ντοκουμεντα *har-tee-ah doh-koo-men-tah*
double διπλο *dip-loh*
down κατω *kah-toh*
drink αναψυκτικο *ah-nahp-sik-tee-koh*
drink, to πινω *pee-noh*
duck παπια *pah-pee-ah*
Dutch Ολλανδος *oh-lahn-dos*

ear αυτι *ahf-tee*
east Ανατολη *ah-nah-toh-lee*
Easter Πασχα *pahs-hah*
easy ευκολο *ef-koh-loh*
eat, to τρωγω *troh-goh*
economical οικονομικο *eeh-koh-noh-mee-ko*
education ανατροφη *ah-nah-troh-fee*

EEC ΕΟΚ *eh-oh-keh*
eel χελι *heh-lee*
egg αυγο *av-goh*
eggplant μελιτζανα *meh-lee-tsah-nah*
eggwhite ασπραδι αυγου *ahs-prah-dee av-goo*
egg yolk κροκαδι *kroh-kah-dee*
elegant κομψος *komp-sos*
elevator ανελκυστηρας *ah-nel-kis-tee-ras*
embassy πρεσβεια *pres-vee-ah*
embers καρβουνα *kahr-voo-nah*
end τελος *teh-los*
England Αγγλια *ah-glee-ah*
Englishman Αγγλος *ah-glos*
Englishwoman Αγγλία *ah-glee-tha*
enough αρκετα *ahr-keh-tah*
enter, to εισερχομαι *ee-ser-hoh-meh*
entrance εισοδος *ees-soh-dos*
entrance εισοδος *is-soh-dos*
envelope φακελος *fah-keh-los*
equal ομοιος *oh-mee-os*
error λαθος *lah-thos*
eternal αιωνιος *eh-oh-nee-os*
European Ευρωπαιος *ev-roh-peh-os*

every καθε *kah-theh*
evident φανερος *fah-neh-ros*
ex πρωην Ο *proh-in*
excellence εξοχοτητα *ex-oh-hoh-tee-tah*
excellent πολυ καλο *poh-lee kah-loh*
excessive υπερβολικο *ee-per-vol-ee-koh*
excursion εκδρομη *ek-droh-mee*
exit εξοδος *ex-oh-doos*
expert εμπειρογνωμον *em-bee-rohg-noh-mon*
extract υπολοιμα *ee-poh-lee-mah*
extreme ακραιος *ah-kreh-os*
eye ματι *mah-tee*

fainted λιποθυμος *lee-poh-thee-mohs*
fall, to πεφτω *pef-toh*
family οικογενεια *ee-koh-yeh-nee-ah*
far μακρια *mah-kree-ah*
fat, grease λιπος *lee-pos*, παχυς *pah-heets*
February Φεβρουαριος *fev-roo-ah-ree-os*
fettuccine χυλοπιτες *hee-loh-pee-tes*
fig συκο *see-koh*
fillet φιλετο *fee-leh-toh*

filter, to διυλιζω *dee-ee-lee-zoh*
find, to ευρισκω *ev-ris-koh*
finish, to τελειωνω *teh-lee-oh-noh*
fire φωτια *foh-tee-ah*
fish ψαρι *psah-ree*
fish (wrapped and steamed) ψαρι στη λαδοκολα *psah-ree stee lah-doh-koh-lah*
fish soup ψαροσουπα *psah-roh-soo-pah*
flame φλογα *floh-gah*
flight πτηση *ptis-see*
flour αλευρι *ah-lev-ree*
fly (insect) μυιγα *mee-gah*
food τροφη *troh-fee*
foodstuffs τρωφιμα *troh-fee-mah* εδωδιμα *eh-doh-dee-mah*
for για *yah*
forget, to ξεχνω *kseh-noh*
France Γαλλια *gal-lee-ah*
frankfurter λουκανικο *loo-kah-nee-koh*
French (adj.) γαλλικος *gal-lee-kos*
French fries τσιπς *tsips*
Frenchman Γαλλος *gal-los*
fresh φρεσκο *fres-koh*
Friday Παρασκευη *pah-rahs-keh-vee*
fried food τηγανισμα *tee-gah-nis-mah*

fried τηγανιτο *tee-gah-nee-toh*
friend φιλος *fee-los*
fritters τηγανιτες *tee-gah-nee-tes*
frog βατραχι *vah-trah-hee*
frozen κατεψυγμενο *kah-tep-sig-meh-noh*
fruit φρουτο *froo-toh*
fruit salad φρουτοσαλατα *froo-toh-sah-lah-tah*
game κυνηγι *kee-nee-yee*
garden κηπος *kee-pos*
garlic σκορδο *skor-doh*
German Γερμανος *yer-mah-nos*
Germany Γερμανια *yer-mah-nee-ah*
gherkins αγγουρακια *ah-goo-rah-kee-ah*
ginger τζιντζερ *zin-zer*
give, to δινω *dee-noh*
glass (material) γυαλι *yah-lee*
glass (small) ποτηρακι *poh-tee-rah-kee*
glass ποτηρι *poh-tee-ree*
go, to πηγαινω *pee-yeh-noh*
goat's cheese κεφαλοτυρι *keh-fah-loh-tee-ree*
gold χρυσος *hris-sos*
golden ροδοκοκκινισμενο *roh-doh-koh-kee-nis-meh-noh*

good καλο *kah-loh*
goose χηνα *hee-nah*
gorgonzola ροκφορ τυρι *rok-for tee-ree*
grain σιταρι *see-tah-ree*
grapes σταφυλι *stah-fee-lee*
grated (minced) τριμμενο *tree-meh-noh*
Great Britain Μεγαλη Βρεττανια *meh-gah-lee vret-tah-nee-ah*
Greece Ελλας *el-las*
Greek (man) Ελληνας *eh-lee-nas*
Greek (woman) Ελληνιδα *eh-lee-nee-dah*
green πρασινο *prahs-see-noh*
grilled στη σχαρα *stee skhah-rah*
group leader αρχηγος *ahr-hee-gos*
guide οδηγος *oh-dee-gos*

hake ινισκος (ψαρι) *ee-nis-kos (psah-ree)*
ham χοιρομερι *hee-roh-meh-ree*
hand χερι *heh-ree*
handkerchief μαντηλι *mahn-dee-lee*
hard σκληρος *sklee-ros*
hare λαγος *lah-gos*
harmless αβλαβης *av-lah-vees*

have, to εχω *eh-hoh*
hazelnuts φουντουκια *foon-doo-kyah*
he αυτος *ahf-tos*
heavy βαρυ *vah-ree*
help, to βοηθω *voh-ee-thoh*
hen κοτα *koh-tah*
here εδω *eh-doh*
herring ρεγγα *reh-gah*
holiday διακοπες *dee-ah-koh-pes*
Holland Ολλανδια *oh-lahn-thee-ah*
honey μελι *meh-lee*
hors-d'oeuvre ορεκτικα *oh-rek-tee-kah*
hospital νοσοκομειο *nos-soh-koh-mee-oh*
hot (spicy) καυτερο *kahf-teh-roh*
hot ζεστη *zes-tee*
hotel ξενοδοχειο *kseh-noh-thoh-hee-oh*
hour ωρα *oh-rah*
house σπιτι *spee-tee*
housewife νοικοκυρα *nee-koh-kee-rah*
how much οσο *os-soh* τοσο *tos-soh* ποσο; *pos-soh?*
how πω οπως *oh-pos*
humid υγρος *ee-grohs*
hunger πεινα *pee-nah*
hunter κυνηγος *kee-nee-gos*
hurry βιασυνη *vyahs-see-nee*

husband συζυγος *oh see-zee-gos*

ice παγος *pah-gos,* παγακια *pah-gah-kyah*
ice-cream παγωτο *pah-goh-toh*
ice-cream parlor παγωτοπωλειο *pah-gah-toh-poh-lee-oh*
identity card ταυτοτητα *tahf-toh-tee-tah*
impossible αδυνατον *ah-dee-nah-ton*
in front εμπρος *em-bros*
in two days σε δυο ημερες *seh dee-oh ee-meh-res*
inform, to πληροφορω *plee-roh-foh-roh*
infusion αφεψημα *ah-fep-see-mah*
inn ουζερι *oo-zeh-ree*
inn ταβερνα *tah-ver-nah*
insect εντομο *en-doh-moh*
inside μεσα *mes-sah*
instead αντι *ahn-dee*
invoice νομικη αποδειξη Ο *noh-mee-kee ah-poh-dix-ee*
Ireland Ιρλανδια *ir-lahn-dee-ah*
iron σιδηρος *see-dee-ros*
Italian (adj.) ιταλικα *ee-tah-lee-kah*
Italian (man) Ιταλος *ee-tah-los* **(woman)** Ιταλιδα *ee-tah-lee-dah*
Italy Ιταλια *ee-tah-lee-ah*

jam μαρμελαδα *mahr-meh-lah-dah*
January Ιανουαριος *ee-ah-noo-ah-ree-os*
jazz τζαζ *zaaz*
jeans τζην *zinn*
jeep τζιπ *zeep*
Jewish (man) Εβραιος *ev-reh-os* **(woman)** Ευβρεα *ev-reah*
jockey τζοκευ *zoh-kei*
jolly μπαλαντερ *bah-lah-der*
jug κανατα *kah-nah-tah*
juice χυμος *hee-mos*
July Ιουλιος *ee-oo-lee-os*
June Ιουνιος *ee-oo-nee-os*

kaki λωτο φρουτα *loh-toh froo-tah*
kid (young goat) κατσικι *kaht-see-kee*
kidney νεφρια *neh-free-ah*
kimono κιμονο *kee-moh-noh*
kiwi κιουι *kee-wee*
know, to γνωριζω *gnoh-ri-zoh*
label ετικετα *eh-tee-keh-tah*
laboratory εργαστηριο *er-gahs-tee-ree-oh*
lake λιμνη *lim-nee*

lamb (χυλ.) αρνακι *ahr-<u>nah</u>-kee*
lamb (roasted) αρνακι φουρνου *ahr-<u>nah</u>-kee <u>foor</u>-noo*
lamb αρνι *ahr-<u>nee</u>*
Larissa Λαρισα *<u>lah</u>-ris-sah*
Larnaca Λαρνακα *<u>lar</u>-nah-kah*
last τελευταιος *teh-lef-<u>teh</u>-ohs*
lean απαχο *ah-pah-hoh*
least (at) τουλαχιστο *too-<u>lah</u>-is-toh*
leave, to αναχωρω *ah-nah-hoh-<u>roh</u>*
leeks πρασα *<u>prahs</u>-sah*
legumes οσπρια *<u>os</u>-pree-ah*
lemon λεμονι *leh-<u>moh</u>-nee*
lemonade λεμοναδα *leh-moh-<u>nah</u>-dah*
lens φακος *fah-<u>kos</u>*
lentils φακες *fah-<u>kes</u>*
Lesbos Λεσβος *<u>les</u>-vos* Μυτιληνη *mee-tee- <u>lee</u>-nee*
less λιγοτερο *lee-<u>goh</u>-teh-roh*
lettuce μαρουλι *mah-<u>roo</u>-lee*
light φως *fos*
light, to αναβω *ah-<u>nah</u>-voh*
line γραμμη *grah-<u>mee</u>*
bitter (liqueur) πικραμυγδαλο *pik-rah-<u>mig</u>-dah-loh*

liqueur λικερ ποτο *lee-<u>ker</u> poh-<u>toh</u>*
list καταλογος *kah-<u>tah</u>-loh-gos*
liter λιτρο *<u>lee</u>-troh*
Livadia Λιβαδια *lee-vah-dee-<u>ah</u>*
liver συκωτι *see-<u>koh</u>-tee*
lobster αστακος *ahs-tah-<u>kos</u>*
loin καπιστρι *kah-<u>pis</u>-tree*
long μακρυς *mah-<u>kris</u>*
long-distance call υπεραστικη *ee-per-ahs-tee-<u>kee</u>*
look, to κοιταζω *kee-<u>tah</u>-zoh*
lose, to χανω *<u>hah</u>-noh*

macaroons αμυγδαλωτα *ah-mig-dah-loh-<u>tah</u>*
Macedonia Μακεδονια *Mah-keh-doh-<u>nee</u>-ah*
mackerel σκουμπρι *skoo-<u>bree</u>*
macrobiotic μακροβιοτικο *mah-kroh-vee-oh-tee-<u>koh</u>*
maize αραποσιτι *ah-rah-pos-see-tee*, καλαμποκι *kah-lah-<u>boh</u>-kee*
make, to κανω *<u>kah</u>-noh*
Malvasia Μαλβασια *Mahl-vah-<u>see</u>-ah*
management διευθυνση *dee-<u>eft</u>-hin-see*
mandarin μανταρινι *mahn-dah-<u>ree</u>-nee*

March Μαρτιος _mahr-tee-os_

marinated μαρινατο _mah-ree-nah-toh_

marjoram ματζουρανα _mah-zoo-rah-nah_

market αγορα _ah-goh-rah_

Mastic μαστιχα _mahs-tee-hah_

match σπιρτο _speer-toh_

matured (seasoned) σιτεμενο _see-teh-meh-noh_

May Μαιος _mah-ee-os_

mayonnaise μαγιονεζα _mah-yoh-neh-zah_

meal γευμα _yev-mah_

meat κρεας _kreh-ahs_ **minced** κυμας _kee-mahs_

meat sauce σαλτσα _sal-tsah_

meatballs κεφτεδες _kef-teh-des_

medicine φαρμακο _fahr-mah-koh_

medlar (fruit) μουσμουλα _moos-moo-lah_

meet, to συναντω _see-nahn-doh_

melon πεπονι _peh-poh-nee_

Mikonos Μυκονος _mee-koh-nos_

milk γαλα _gah-lah_

milkshake φραπε _frah-peh_

minced κυμας _kee-mahs_

mint δυοσμος _dee-os-mos_

minute λεπτο _lep-toh_

Miss δεσποινιδα _des-pee-nee-dah_

Mistra Uso Μυστρα Ουζο _mis-trah oo-zoo_

mixed ποικιλια _pee-kee-lee-ah_

mixture μιγμα _mig-mah_

molluscs θαλασσινα _thah-lahs-see-nah_

Monday Δευτερα _def-teh-rah_

month μηνας _mee-nas_

monuments μνημεια _mnee-mee-ah_

morning πρωι _pro-ee_

mortadella μορταδελα _mor-tah-deh-lah_

mosquitoes κουνουπια _koo-noo-pyah_

mother μητερα _mee-teh-rah_

mouth στομα _stoh-mah_

Mr. κυριος _kee-ree-os_

Mrs. κυρια _kee-ree-ah_

much πολυ _poh-lee_

mullet κεφαλος _keh-fah-los_

mullet μπαρμπουνι _bahr-boo-nee_

Muscat Μοσχατο _mos-kah-toh_

museum μουσειο _moos-see-oh_

mushroom μανιταρι _mah-nee-tah-ree_

music μουσικη _moos-see-kee_

name ονομα _oh_-noh-mah
Naxos Ναξος _nah_-ksos
near διπλα _deep_-lah
need αναγκη ah-_nah_-gee
neighborhood, τα περιξ _tah_
  peh-riks
never ποτε poh-_teh_
New Year's Day
  Πρωτοχρονια proh-toh-
  hroh-nee-_ah_
news πληροφορια plee-roh-
  foh-_ree_-ah
newspaper εφημεριδα eh-
  fee-meh-_ree_-dah
newsstand περιπτερο peh-
  reep-teh-roh
Nicosia Λευκωσια lef-kohs-
  see-ah
no οχι _oh_-hee
nobody κανεις kah-_nis_
non-alcoholic αναλκολικο
  ah-nah-al-koh-lee-_koh_
non-smoker οχι καπνιζοντες
  _oh_-hee kahp-_nee_-zon-des
noodles κριθαρακι kree-tha-
  rah-kee
north Βορρας voh-_rahs_
not δεν den
nothing τιποτα _tee_-poh-tah
notice ειδοποιηση ee-doh-
  pee-_iss_-see
November Νοεμβριος noh-
  em-vree-os
number αριθμος ah-rith-_mos_

nutmeg μοσχοκαρυδο mos-
  koh-_kah_-ree-doh

oasis οαση _oh_-ah-see
oats βρωμη _vroh_-mee
obligatory υποχρεωτικο ee-
  pohreh-oh-tee-_koh_
obtain, to αποκτω ah-pok-
  toh
October Οκτωβριος ok-_toh_-
  vree-os
offal σπληναντερο splee-
  nahn-deh-roh
often συχνα seh-_nah_
oil λαδι _lah_-dee
olive ελια eh-lee-_ah_
Olympus Ολυμπος _oh_-lim-
  bos
onion κρεμμυδι kreh-_mee_-
  dee
open ανοικτο ah-nik-_toh_
open-air εξω _ek_-soh
orange πορτοκαλι por-toh-
  kah-lee
orangeade πορτοκαλαδα
  por-toh-kah-_lah_-dah
order παραγγελια pah-rah-
  geh-_lee_-ah
order, to παραγγελω pah-
  rah-_geh_-loh
oregano ριγανη _ree_-gah-nee
other αλλο _ahl_-loh
out εξω _ex_-hoh
out of order βλαβη _vlah_-vee

outside εξωτερικος *ex-oh-teh-ree-kos*
ox βοδι *voh-dee*
oysters στρειδια *stree-dee-ah*

pair δυο *dee-oh*
pan τηγανι *tee-ghah-nee*
paper χαρτι *hahr-tee*
paper tissue χαρτομανδηλο *har-toh-man-dee-loh*
parents γονεις *goh-nees*
park παρκο *pahr-koh*
Parmesan (cheese) παρμιτζανα *pahr-mee-zah-na*
parsley μαιντανος *mah-in-dah-nos*
party γιορτη *yee-or-tee*
passport διαβατηριο *dee-ah-vah-tee-ree-oh*
pasta μακαροναδα *mah-kah-roh-nah-dah*
pastries παστες *pahs-tes*
pastry (puff) παστα σφολια *pahs-tah sfoh-lee-ah*
pastry (shortcrust) παστα μπριζε *pahs-tah bree-zeh*
pastry shop ζαχαροπλαστειο *zah-hah-roh-plahs-tee-oh*
pastry ζυμαρικα *zee-mah-ree-kah*
pay, to πληρωνω *plee-roh-noh*
payment πληρωμη *plee-roh-mee*

peanut φυστικι αραπικο *fis-tee-kee ah-rah-pee-koh*
pear αχλαδι *ah-lah-dee*
peas αρακας *ah-rah-kas*
peel, to ξεφλουδιζω *kseh-floo-di-zoh*
Peloponnese Πελοπονησος *peh-loh-poh-nis-sos*
pen πενα *pen-nah*
pepper πιπερι *pee-peh-ree*
pepper-mill μυλος για πιπερι *mee-los yah pee-peh-ree*
peppers (cooked) πιπεριες γιαχνι *pee-peh-ree-es yah-nee*
perhaps ισως *ees-sohs*
permit αδεια *ah-dee-ah*
pharmacy φαρμακειο *far-mah-kee-oh*
pheasant φασιανος *fas-see-ah-nos*
pickles τουρσι *toor-see*
pineapple ανανας *ah-nah-nas*
pistachio nuts φυστικια *fis-tee-kee*
pizza (stuffed) μπουρεκακια *boo-reh-kah-kee-ah*
place, club χωρος *hoh-ros*, κεντρο διασκεδασεως *ken-droh dee-ahs- keh-das-seh-os*
play, to παιζω *peh-zoh*
plaza πλατεια *plah-tee-ah*

please παρακαλω *pah-rah-kah-loh*

plums δαμασκινα *dah-mahs-kee-nah*

polyp (octopus) χταποδι *htah-poh-dee*

pork χοιρινο *hee-ree-noh*

portion μεριδα *meh-ree-thah*

pot κατσαρολα *kat-tsah-roh-lah*

potato πατατα *pah-tah-tah*

pregnant εγκυος *eh-gee-os*

preservatives διατυριντικα *dee-ah-tee-rin-dee-kah*

price τιμη *tee-mee*

pudding πουτιγκα *poo-tee-gah*

pulp ψαχνο *psah-noh*

pumpkin κολοκυθα *koh-loh-kee-thah*

quail ορτυκι *ohr-tee-kee*

quality ποιοτητα *pee-oh-tee-tah*

quantity ποσοτητα *pos-soh-tee-tah*

quarter τεταρτο *teh-tar-toh*

question ερωτηση *eh-roh-tis-see* ζητημα *zee-tee-mah*

quotient δεικτης *dik-tis*

rabbit κουνελι *koo-neh-lee*

radish ραπανακι *rah-pah-nah-kee*

raisins σταφιδα *stah-fee-dah*

raspberries σμεουρα *smeh-oo-rah*

read, to διαβαζω *dee-ah-va-zoh*

receipt αποδειξη *ah-poh-dix-see*

recipe συνταγη *sin-dah-yee*

red κοκκινος *koh-kee-nos*, ερυθρος *eh-ree-thros*

reef σκοπελος *skoh-peh-los*

refrigerator ψυγειο *psee-yee-oh*

refund αποδοση *ah-poh-thos-see*

region νομος *noh-mos*

rental ενοικιο *eh-nee-kee-oh*

reply, to απαντω *ah-pahn-doh*

reserve, to κρατω *krah-toh* κλεινω *klee-noh*

reserved ρεσερβε *reh-ser-veh*

restaurant εστιατοριο *es-tee-ah-toh-ree-oh*

Rhodes Ροδος *roh-dos*

rhubarb ραβεντι *rah-ven-dee*

rice ρυζι *ri-zee*

ricotta cheese μανουρι *mah-noo-ree*, μυζηθρα *mi-zee-trah*

right δεξια *dex-see-ah*

right ευθεια *ef-thee-ah*

ripe ωριμος *oh-ree-mos*

roast fish ψαρι ψητο _psah-ree psee-toh_
roast ψητο φουρνου _psee-toh foor-noo_
roasted ξεροψημενο _kseh-rop-see-meh-noh_
rocket salad γλιστριδα _glis-tree-dah_
rolls (stuffed meat) ντολμαδακια _dol-mah-dak-yah_ ντολμαδες _dol-mah-des_
rolls μπουρεκακια _boo-reh-kah-kee-ah_
room δωματιο _doh-mah-tee-oh_
root ριζα _ri-zah_
rôtisserie ψητοπωλειο _psee-toh-poh-lee-oh_ ψησταρια _psis-tah-ree-ah_
rump ψαχνο _psah-noh_
runner beans φασολακια _fah-soh-lah-kyah_

salad σαλατα _sah-lah-tah_
salami σαλαμι _sah-lah-mee_
Salamina Σαλαμινα _sah-lah-mee-nah_
salmon σολομος _soh-loh-mos_
salt αλατι _ah-lah-tee_
salty αλμυρο _ahl-mee-roh_
same το ιδιο _toh ee-dee-oh_
Samos Σαμος _sah-mohs_
sand αμμος _ahm-mos_
sardine σαρδελες _sahr-deh-les_

Saturday Σαββατο _sah-vah-toh_
sauce σαλτσα _sal-tsah_
sauce less χωρις σαλτσα _hoh-ris sahl-tsah_
sausage σουτζουκια _soo-zoo-kyah_
say, to λεγω _leh-goh_
sea θαλασσα _thah-lahs-sah_
seabream τσιπουρα _tsee-poo-rah_
seafood θαλασσινα _thah-lahs-see-nah_
season εποχη _eh-poh-hee_
sedative ηρεμιστικο _ee-reh-mis-tee-koh_
see, to βλεπω _vleh-poh_
semolina σιμιγδαλι _see-mig-dah-lee_
September Σεπτεμβριος _sep-tem-vree-os_
set, to (table) στρωστε το τραπεζι _stros-teh toh trah-peh-zee_
share μερτικο _mer-tee-koh_
shaved ice γρανιτα _grah-nee-tah_
shell κελιφος _keh-lee-fos_
show, to δειχνω _deeh-noh_
shrimp γαριδακια _gah-ree-dah-kee-ah_
sick, ill αρρωστος _ah-ros-tos_
signature υπογραφη _ee-poh-grah-fee_

site μερος _meh-ros_
skewers σουβλακια _soov-lah-kyah_
small μικρος _mee-kros_
smell μυρωδια _mee-roh-dee-ah_
smoked καπνιστος _kap-nis-tos_
snails σαλιγκαρια _sah-lee-gah-ree-ah_
sole γλωσσα _glos-sah_
some μερικοι _meh-ree-kee_
something κατι _khah-tee_
son γυιος _yee-os_
song τραγουδι _trah-goo-dee_
soup σουπα _soo-pah_
sour αγουρο _ah-goo-roh_
south Νοτος _noh-tos_
spaghetti σπαγετι _spah-yeh-tee_
spices μπαχαρικα _bah-hah-ree-kah_
spinach σπανακια _spah-nah-kyah_
spirits οινοπνευματωδη _ee-nop-nev-mah-toh-dee_
squid σουπια _soo-pee-ah_
squid καλαμαρια _kah-lah-mah-ree-ah_

stamp (postage) γραμματοσημο _grah-mah-tos-see-moh_
starch αμυλο _ah-mee-loh_

station σταθμος _stath-mohs_
stay, to παραμενω _pah-rah-meh-noh_
steak (grilled) μπριζολα στη σχαρα _brit-zoh-lah stee skhah-rah_
steak μπριζολα _brit-zoh-lah_
steam ατμος _aht-mohs_
still (yet, again) ακομη _ah-koh-mee_
stop σταση _stahs-see_
stop, to σταματω _stah-mah-toh_
store, shop μαγαζι _mah-ghat-zee_
strawberry φραουλα _frah-oo-lah_
street δρομος _droh-mohs_
stuffed γεμιστο _yeh-mis-toh_
style τροπος _troh-pos_
sugar ζαχαρη _zah-hah-ree_
sugarbowl ζαχαριερα _zah-hah-ree-eh-rah_
summer (adj.) καλοκαιρινος _kah-loh-keh-ree-nos_
summer καλοκαιρι _kah-loh-keh-ree_
Sunday Κυριακη _kee-ree-ah-kee_
supper δειπνο _dip-noh_
surname επιθετο _eh-pee-theh-toh_
sweet γλυκος _glee-kos_

sweet-and-sour γλυκοξινο
  glee-_koks_-ee-noh
sweets λιχουδιες lee-hoo-
  dee-_es_
swim, to κολυμβω koh-lim-
  boh
Switzerland Ελβετια el-veh-
  tee-ah
swordfish ξιφιας ksee-_fee_-ahs

table τραπεζι trah-_pe_-zee
tablecloth τραπεζομανδηλο
  trah-peh-zoh-_mahn_-dee-loh
tablet χαπι _hah_-pee
tagliatelle χυλοπιτες hee-
  loh-_pee_-tes
talcum powder ταλκ tahlk
taste γουστο _goos_-toh γευση
  yef-see
taste, to δοκιμαζω doh-kee-
  _ma_-zoh
tea τσαϊ _tsah_-ee
tender τρυφερος tree-feh-_ros_
terminus αφετηρια ah-feh-
  teh-_ree_-ah
thank, to ευχαριστω ehf-
  hah-ris-_toh_
thanks ευχαριστω ef-hah-ris-
  toh
that εκεινο eh-_kee_-noh
that τι tee
the η ee
there εκει eh-_kee_
thigh μπουτι _boo_-tee

thirst διψα dip-sah
this αυτο ahf-_toh_
thread κλωστη kloh-_stee_
throat λαιμος leh-_mos_
Thursday Πεμπτη _pemp_-tee
ticket εισιτηριο iss-see-_tee_-
  ree-oh
time χρονος _hroh_-nos
tin-pener ανοικτιρι
  κουτιου ah-nik-_tee_-ree
  koo-tee-_oo_
tip φιλοδωριμα fee-loh-_doh_-
  ree-mah
tobacconist καπνοπωλειο
  kahp-noh-poh-_lee_-oh
today σημερα _see_-meh-rah
together μαζι mah-_zee_
toilet αποχωρητηριο ah-poh-
  hoh-ree-_tee_-ree-oh
tomatoes (stuffed with rice)
  ντοματες γεμιστες doh-
  mah-tes yeh-mis-_tes_
tomorrow αυριο _av_-ree-oh
tongue, language γλωσσα
  glos-sah
tonight αποψε ah-_pop_-seh
tooth δοντι _don_-dee
toothpick οδοντογλυφιδα oh-
  don-doh-glee-_fee_-dah
total ολοκληρος oh-_lok_-lee-
  ros
tour γυρος _yee_-ros
towel πετσετα pet-_seh_-ta
train τραινο _treh_-noh

transport μεταφορικο μεσο
meh-tah-foh-ree-*koh* mes-
soh
tray δισκος *dis*-kos
tripe πατσας paht-*sahs*
trout πεστροφα *pehs*-troh-
fah
Tuesday Τριτη *tree*-tee
tunafish τονος ψαρι *toh*-nos
psah-ree
turkey γαλοπουλα gah-loh-
poo-lah

ugly ασχημος *ah*-shee-mos
United States of America
Ηνωμενες Πολιτειες
Αμερικής ee-noh-*meh*-nehs
Poh-lee-*tee*-es ahm-eh-ree-
kees
understand, to καταλαβαινω
kah-tah-lah-*veh*-noh
use, to χρησιμοποιω hris-
see-moh-pee-*oh*

vanilla βανιλια vah-*nee*-lyah
VAT Φ.Π.Α fee-pee-*ah*
veal μοσχαρι mohs-*kah*-ree
veal rump ψαχνο μοσχαρι
psah-*noh* mos-*khah*-ree
vegetable garden
λαχανοκηπος lah-hah-*noh*
kee-pos
vegetable hors-oeuvre
ορεκτικα ζαρζαβατικα oh-

rek-tee-*kah* zar-zah-vah-tee-
kah
vegetable soup χορτοσουπα
hor-*toh*-soo-pah
vegetables λαχανικα lah-
hah-nee-*kah*
vegetables γαρνιτουρα gahr-
nee-*too*-rah
vegetarian χορτοφαγος hor-
toh-*fah*-gos
vermicelli φιδες fee-*de*
view αποψη *ah*-pop-see
vinegar ξυδι *ksee*-dee
vintage (year) χρονια hroh-
nee-*ah*

wait, to περιμενω peh-ree-
meh-noh
waiter σερβιτορος ser-vee-
toh-ros
walk, to βαδιζω vah-*dee*-soh
walnuts καρυδια kah-*ree*-
dyah
want, to θελω *theh*-loh
wardrobe γκαρνταρομπα
gahr-dah-roh-bah
warn, to ειδοποιω ee-doh-
pee-*oh*
wash, to πλενω *pleh*-noh
water νερο neh-*roh*
watermelon καρπουζι kahr-
poo-zee
waterproof αδιαβροχο ad-
yahv-roh-hoh

weak αδυνατος *ah-dee-nah-tos*

weather καιρος *keh-ros*

Wednesday Τεταρτη *teh-tar-tee*

week εβδομαδα *ev-doh-mah-dah*

weekday εργασιμη ημερα *er-gass-see-mee ee-meh-rah*

welcome καλωσοριστε *kah-los-soh-ris-teh*

well καλα *kah-lah*

west δυτικα *dee-tee-kah*

when οταν *oh-tan* ποτε; *poh-teh?*

where που; *poo?* οπου *oh-poo*

wherever παντου *pahn-doo*

which οποιο *oh–pee–o* ποιο *pee-oh*

while ενω *eh-noh*

white ασπρο *ahs-proh*

who ποιος *pee-ohs*, οποιος *oh-pee-ohs*

wholemeal (bread) ψωμι μαυρο *psoh-mee mahv-roh*

why, because γιατι *yah-tee*

wife η συζυγος *ee see-zee-gos*

window παραθυρο *pah-rah-tee-roh*

wine κρασι *krahs-see*

winter χειμωνας *hee-moh-nahs*

with με *meh*

without διχως *dee-hos*

woman γυναικα *yee-neh-kah*

word λεξις *lek-sis*

work εργασια *er-gahs-see-ah*

year χρονος *hroh–nos*

yellow κιτρινο *kee-tree-noh*

yesterday εχθες *eh-thes*

yoghurt γιαουρτι *yah-oor-tee*

young νεος *neh-os* νεαρος *neh-ah-ros*

Yugoslav Γιουγκοσλαβος *yoo-gohs-lah-vos*

zucchini κολοκυθακια *koh-loh-kee-thah-kyah*

αγγουρι *ah-goo-ree* n.
cucumber

αγκαθι *ah-ghah-thee* n.
draught

αγκιναρα *agh-ee-nah-rah* f.
artichoke

αγκιναρες αυγολεμονο *agh-
ee-nah-res av-goh-leh-moh-
noh* see "National Dishes"
p. 31

αγκιναρες με αρακα *agh-ee-
nah-res meh ahr-ah-kah* see
"National Dishes" p. 31

αγκιναρες με αρνακι *agh-ee-
nah-res meh ahr-nah-kee*
see "National Dishes" p. 32

Αγκιναρες με κρεας,
αυγολεμονο *agh-ghee-nah-
res meh kreh-ahs av-goh-
leh-moh-noh* see "Recipes"
p. 59

αγκιστρι *ah-gees-tree* n. hook

αγορα *ah-goh-rah* f. market,
purchase

αγοραζω *ah-goh-rah-zoh* v.
to buy

αγουρος *ah-goo-ros* adj.
bitter

αγριοκατσικο *ah-gree-oh-
kaht-tsee-koh* n. suède, wild
kid

αγριοπαπια *ah-gree-oh-pah-
pyah* f. wild duck

αγριοπαπια σαλμι *ah-gree-
oh pah-pyah sahl-mee* duck
in salmì, see "Regional
Dishes" p. 45

αγροικια *ah-gree-kee-ah* f.
farm, dairy

αγροτης *ah-groh-tis* m.
farmer

αδειος *ah-dee-os* adj. empty

αερισμος *ah-ehr-is-mos* m.
ventilation

αηδιασσικος *ay-dee-as-tee-
kohs* disgusting

αθικτος *ah-thik-tos* adj.
intact

αθροισμα *ah-thris-mah* n.
addition

αιθουσα *eh-thoos-sah* f. hall,
room

αιθουσα αναμονης *eh-
thoos-sah ah-nah-moh-nees*,
waiting room

αιμα *eh-mah* n. blood

αισθανομαι *es-thah -noh-
meh* v. to feel

ακαθαρτος *ah-khah-thar-tos*
adj. dirty

αλατι *ah-lah-tee* n. salt

αλατοπιπερο *ah-lah-toh-pee-
peh-roh* n. salt and pepper

αλευρι *ah-leh-vree* n. flour

αλλαντικα διαφορα *ahl-
lahn-dee-kah dee-ah-foh-
rah* see "Sausages and Cold
Cuts" p. 15

αμπελι *ahm-beh-lee* n. vineyard

αμπελοφασουλα *ahm-beh-loh-fah-soo-lah* n. pl. wide, flat greenbeans

αμπελοφυλλα *ahm-beh-loh-fil-lah* pl. vine leaves, see "Other Specialties" p. 29

αμυγδαλο *ah-mig-dah-loh* n. almond, see also "Other Specialties" p. 29

αμυγδαλωτα *ah-migh-dah-loh-tah* biscuits (almond paste), see "Sweets" p. 21

αμυγδαλωτα Υδραϊκα *ah-migh-dah-loh-tah Ee-drey-kah* see "Sweets" p. 21 and "Recipes" p. 68

αν *ahn* conj. if

αναγκη *ah-nah-ghee* f. need

αναγουλα *ah-nah-goo-lah* f. nausea

ανακαλυψη *ah-nah-kah-lip-see* f. uncovered

ανακατευω *ah-nah-kah-teh-voh* v. to mix, stir

ανακοινωση *ah-nah-kee-nos-see* f. announcement

ανανας *ah-nah-nahs* m. pineapple

αναπηρος *ah-nah-pee-ros* adj. disabled

αναχωρηση *ah-nah-hoh-ris-see* f. departure

αναψυκτικο *ah-nap-sik-tee-koh* n. drink

ανεση *ah-nes-see* f. comfort

ανηλικος *ah-nee-lee-kos* m. a minor

ανθοτυρο *an-thoh-tee-roh* see "Cheeses" p. 17

ανθογαλα *an-thoh-gah-lah* n. cream see "Other Specialties" p. 29

ανθος λεμονιας *an-thos leh-moh-nee-as* f. lemon blossom jam see "Regional Dishes" p. 55

ανθρωπος *an-throh-pos* m. man, person

ανιθο *ah-nee-thoh* n. dill, see "Other Specialties" p. 29

ανοιξη *ah-nik-see* f. spring

ανοιχτηρι κουτιου *ah-nih-tee-ree koo-tee-oo* n. can-opener

ανοιχτος *ah-nih-tos* adj. open

αντζουγια *an-zoo-yah* f. anchovy

αντιβιοτικο *an-dee-vee-oh-tee-koh* n. antibiotic

αντιδια *an-dee-dyah* n. endive

απαγορευεται η εισοδος *ah-pah-goh-reh-veh-teh ee ees-soh-dos* no entry απογειωση *ah-poh ghee-os-see* f. take-off

αποδειξη *ah-poh-deex-see* f. receipt

αποδοση χρηματων *ah-poh-dos-see hree-mah-ton* f. reimbursement

απορρυπαντικο *ah-poh-ree-pahn-dee-koh* n. detergent

αποσκευη *ah-poh-skeh-vee* f. baggage

αποσταση *ah-pohs-tahs-see* f. distance

αποχωρηση *ah-poh-hoh-riss-see* f. retreat

αποχωρητηριο *ah-poh-hoh-ree-tee-ree-oh* n. restroom

αποψε *ah-pop-seh* adv. tonight

Απριλιος *ah-pree-lee-os* m. April

απων *ah-pohn* adj. absent

Αραβας *ah-rah-vahs* m. Arab

αρακας *ah-rah-kahs* m. spring peas

αρακας με αγκιναρες *ah-rah-kahs meh ah-ghee-nah-res* see "National Dishes" p. 32

αρακας με κρεας *ah-rah-kahs meh kreh-ahs* peas with meat , see "National Dishes" p. 32 and "Recipes" p. 60

αραποσιτι *ah-rah-pos-see-tee* n. maize

αργοπορια *ar-goh-poh-ree-ah* f. delay

αριθμος *ar-rith-mohs* n. number

αριστερα *ah-ris-teh-rah* adv. left

Αρκαδια *ar-kah-dee-ah* see "Wines" p. 24

αρκετα *ar-keh-tah* adv. enough

αρμυρος *ar-mee-ros* adj. salted

αρνακι κλεφτικο *ar-nah-kee klef-tee-koh* spring lamb with vegetables, see "Regional Dishes" p. 48

αρνακι λεμονατο *ar-nah-kee leh-moh-nah-toh,* spring lamb with lemon, see "Regional Dishes" p. 49

αρνακι σουβλας *ahr-nah-kee soov-lahs* lamb on the spit, see "National Dishes" p. 32

αρνακι σπιτισιο *ahr-nah-kee spee-tees-see-oh* lamb in tomato sauce, see "National Dishes" p. 32

αρνακι φουρνου *ahr-nah-kee foor-noo,* baked lamb, see "National Dishes" p. 32

αρνι γαλακτος *ar-nee gah-lak-tos* n. spring lamb

αρνι γιουβετσι ar-_nee_ yoo-_vet_-tsee see "Recipes" p. 61

αρνι εξοχικο ar-_nee_ ex-oh-hee-_koh_ country-style lamb, see "National Dishes" p. 33

αρνι σουβλακια ar-_nee_ soov-_lah_-kyah see "Recipes" p. 66

αρνι φρικασε ar-_nee_ free-kahs-_seh_ see "National Dishes" p. 33 and "Recipes" p. 67

αρτοποιειο ar-toh-pee-_oh_ n. bakery

αρωμα _ah_-roh-mah n. smell

ασανσερ ahs-sahn-_ser_ n. elevator

ασημι ahs-_see_-mee n. silver

ασθενοφορο ahs-teh-noh-_foh_-roh n. ambulance

ασπιρινη ahs-pee-_ree_-nee m. aspirin

ασπρορουχα ahs-_proh_-roo-hah n. linen

αστακος ahs-tah-_kos_ m. lobster

αστακος στα καρβουνα ahs-tah-_kos_ stah _kahr_-voo-nah m. lobster (barbecued), see "Natonal Dishes" p. 33

αστακος ω γκρατεν as-tah-_kos_ oh grah-ten m. lobster au gratin

αστυνομια ahs-tee-noh-_mee_-ah f. police

αστυνομικος ahs-tee-noh-mee-_kos_ m. policeman

αστυφυλακας ahs-tee-fee-_lah_-kahs m. guard

ασφαλεια ahs-_fah_-lee-ah f. insurance

ατζεμ πιλαφ ah-_zem_ pee-_lahf_ risotto with tomato, see "National Dishes" p. 33

ατμος aht-_mohs_ m. steam

ατομικος _ah_-toh-mee-kos adj. individual

ατομο _ah_-toh-moh n. individual

Αττικη aht-tee-_kee_ see "Wines" p. 24

αυγο av-_goh_ n. egg χτυπητο ktee-pee-_toh_ beaten egg βραστο vras-_toh_ hard-boiled egg

αυγολεμονο av-goh-_leh_-moh-noh see "Sauces and Condiments" p. 19

Αυγουστος _av_-goos-tos m. August

αυριο _av_-ree-oh adv. tomorrow

αυριο το πρωι _av_-ree-oh toh pro-_ee_ adv. tomorrow morning

αυτοκινητο af-toh-_kee_-nee-toh n. automobile

αυτοκινητοδρομος af-toh-kee-nee-_toh_-droh-mos m.

highway

αφετηρια *ah-feh-teh-<u>ree</u>-ah* f.
end of the line

αφηνω *ah-<u>fee</u>-noh* v. to leave

αφθονος *af-thoh-nos* adj.
abundant

αφιξη *<u>ah</u>-fix-see* f. arrival

αφου *ah-<u>foo</u>* conj. since, as

αφρος *ah-<u>fros</u>* m. foam, lather

Αχαϊα *ah-hah-<u>ee</u>-ah* see
"Wines" p. 24

αχλαδι *ah-<u>lah</u>-dee* n. pear

βαγονι *vah-<u>goh</u>-nee* n.
carriage

βαζω *<u>vah</u>-zoh* v. to place

βαλιτσα *vah-<u>leet</u>-sah* f.
suitcase

βαμβακι *vahm-<u>vah</u>-kee* n.
cotton

βανιλια *vah-<u>nee</u>-lee-ah* f.
vanilla

βαρος *<u>vah</u>-ros* n. weight

βασιλειο *vahs-<u>see</u>-lee-oh* n.
kingdom

βγαινω *<u>vghe</u>h-noh* v. to exit

βδομαδα *vdoh-<u>mah</u>-dah* f.
week

βεβαιος *<u>veh</u>-veh-os* adj.
certain

βεβαιωνω *veh-veh-<u>oh</u>-noh*
v. to affirm

βελουδο *veh-<u>loo</u>-thoh* n.
velvet

βενζιναδικο *ven-zee-<u>nah</u>-
dee-koh* n. gas station
attendant

βενζινη *ven-<u>zee</u>-nee* f.
gasoline

βενταλια *ven-<u>tah</u>-lee-ah* f.
fan

βεραντα *veh-<u>rahn</u>-dah* f.
verandah

βερυκοκο *veh-<u>ree</u>-koh-koh*
n. apricot

βια *<u>vee</u>-ah* f. violence

βιασυνη *vee-ahs-<u>see</u>-nee* f.
hurry

βιβλιο *viv-<u>lee</u>-oh* n. book

βιβλιοθηκη *viv-lee-oh-<u>thee</u>-
kee* f. library

Βιβλος *<u>veev</u>-los* f. Bible αγια
γραφη *ah-<u>yee</u>-ah* grah-<u>fee</u>
Bible

βιζα *<u>vee</u>-zah* f. view, sight

βιολι *vee-oh-<u>lee</u>* n. violin

βιος *<u>vee</u>-os* m. life

βιταμινη *vee-tah-<u>mee</u>-nee* f.
vitamins

βλαβη *<u>vlah</u>-vee* f. damage

βλεμμα *<u>vleh</u>-mah* n. glance,
look

βοδι *<u>voh</u>-thee* n. beef, ox

βοηθεια *voh-<u>ee</u>-thee-ah* f.
help

Βορρας *voh-<u>ras</u>* m. North

βοσκος *vos-<u>kos</u>* m. shepherd,
pastor

βοτανι voh-<u>tah</u>-nee n.
medicinal plants

βουνο voo-<u>noh</u> n. mountain

βουτυρο <u>voo</u>-tee-roh n.
butter

βραδια vrah-dee-<u>ah</u> f.
evening performance

βραδυ <u>vrah</u>-dee n. evening

βραζω <u>vrah</u>-zoh v. boil, to

βραστος <u>vras</u>-tos adj.
stewed, boiled

βρεχω <u>vreh</u>-hoh v. soak, to

βρισκω <u>vris</u>-koh v. find, to

βροχη vroh-<u>hee</u> f. rain

βρυση <u>vris</u>-see f. fountain,
tap

βρωμικος <u>vroh</u>-mee-kos adj.
dirty

βυσσινο <u>vis</u>-see-noh n. black
cherry see also "Other
Specialties" p. 29

γαβαθα gah-<u>vah</u>-thah f. bowl

γαλα <u>gah</u>-lah n. milk

γαλα συμπυκνωμενο <u>gah</u>-lah
sim-bik-noh-<u>meh</u>-noh n.
condensed milk

γαλακτομπουρεκο gah-lak-
toh-<u>boo</u>-reh-koh see
"Sweets" p. 21

γαλακτοπωλειο gah-lak-toh-
poh-<u>lee</u>-oh n. dairy

γαλλικος gah-lee-<u>kos</u> adj.
French

γαλοπουλα gah-loh-<u>poo</u>-lah
f. turkey

γαλοπουλα γεμιστη gah-loh-
<u>poo</u>-lah yeh-mis-<u>tee</u> stuffed
turkey see "National
Dishes" p. 33

γαμος <u>gah</u>-mos m. wedding

γαριδα gah-<u>ree</u>-dah f.
crayfish

γαριδες βραστες gah-<u>ree</u>-
des vrahs-<u>tes</u> f. stewed
crayfish, see "National
Dishes" p. 33

γαριδες με φετα gah-<u>ree</u>-des
meh <u>feh</u>-tah f. crayfish and
cheese, see "National
Dishes" p. 33

γαριδες σαγανακι gah-<u>ree</u>-
des sah-gah-<u>nah</u>-kee f. pan-
cooked crayfish, see
"Regional Dishes" p. 57

γαριδες τηγανητες gah-<u>ree</u>-
des tee-gah-nee-<u>tes</u> f. fried
crayfish, see "National
Dishes" p. 34

γαρνιτουρα gahr-nee-<u>too</u>-rah
f. vegetables

γαστριτιδα gahs-<u>tree</u>-tee-dah
f. gastritis

γαστρονομικος gahs-troh-
noh-<u>mee</u>-kos adj.
gastronomic

γατος <u>gah</u>-tos m. cat

γαυρος <u>gav</u>-ros m. anchovy

γδυνω _gdee-noh_ v. to peel, to skin

γεγονος _yeh-goh-nos_ n. event

γεια σας _yah-sahs_ interj. Hi!

γειτονας _yee-toh-nas_ m. neighbor

γελιο _yeh-lee-oh_ n. laughter

γελω _yeh-loh_ v. to laugh

γεματος _yeh-mah-tos_ adj. full

γεμιζω _yeh-mee-zoh_ v. fill, to

γεμιστος _yeh-mis-tohs_ adj. stuffed, filled

γενεα _yeh-neh-ah_ f. generation

Γερμανος _yer-mah-nos_ m. German (man)

γενιεμαι _yeh-nee-eh-meh_ v. to be born

γενικος _yeh-nee-kos_ adj. general

γεννηση _yeh-nis-see_ f. birth

γερουσια _yeh-roos-see-ah_ f. senate

γευμα _yev-mah_ n. meal

γευματιζω _yev-mah-tee-zoh_ v. dine, to

γευση _yef-see_ f. taste

γευστικος _yef-stee-kohs_ adj. tasty

γεφυρα _yeh-fee-rah_ f. bridge

γεωγραφια _yeh-oh-grah-fee-ah_ f. geography

γεωργια _yeh-ohr-yee-ah_ f. agriculture

γεωργος _yeh-or-gohs_ m. farmer

γη _yee_ f. land

για _yee-ah_ prep. for, until

γιαουρτι _yah-oor-tee_ n. yoghurt

γιαουρτι με μελι _yah-oor-tee meh meh-lee_ n. yoghurt with honey

γιαουρτι σακουλας _yah-oor-tee sah-koo-lahs_ n. concentrated yoghurt

γιατι _yah-tee_ conj. because

γιατρευω _yah-treh-voh_ v. cure, to

γιατρος _yah-tros_ m. doctor

γιαχνι _yah-nee_ stewed

γιδα _yee-dah_ f. goat

γινομαι _yee-noh-meh_ v. to become

γιορτη _yohr-tee_ f. feast, holiday

γιος _yee-os_ m. son

γιουβετσι _yoo-vet-tsee_ n. earthenware, dish see "Regional Dishes" p. 34

Γιουγκοσλαβος _yoo-gohs-lah-vos_ Yugoslav (man)

γιουρβαλακια _yoor-vah-lak-kyah_ n. see "National Dishes" p. 34

γιουσλεμεδες _yoos-leh-meh-des_ m. see "Regional Dishes" p. 57

γκαζι _gah-zee_ n. gas, accelerator

γκαζοζα _gah-zoh-zah_ drink (effervescent)

γκαρσονι _gahr-soh-nee_ n. waiter, valet

γκριζος _gree-zohs_ adj. grey

γκρουπ _groop_ n. group

γλυκα _glee-kah_ f. sweetness

γλυκα _glee-ka_ n. pl. sweets

γλυκα του κουταλιου _glee-kah too koo-tah-lee-oo_ sweets by the spoon, see "Regional Dishes" p. 55

γλυκορριζα _glee-koh-riz-zah_ f. liquorice

γλυκος _glee-kos_ adj. sweet

γλυπτικη _glip-tee-kee_ f. sculpture

γλωσσα _glos-sah_ f. tongue, sole

γνησιος _gnis-see-os_ adj. authentic

γνωμη _gnoh-mee_ f. opinion

γνωριζω _gnor-eet-zoh_ v. to know

γνωρισμα _gnoh-ris-mah_ n. marking

γνωση _gnos-see_ f. knowledge

γονεας _goh-neh-ahs_ m. parent

γοπες τηγανητες με σαβορι _goh-pes tee-gah-nee-tes meh sah-voh-ree_ fried fish, see "Regional Dishes" p. 57

γουρουνι _goo-roo-nee_ n. pork

γουρουνοπουλο με κολοκασι _goo-roo-noh-poo-loh meh koh-loh-kahs-see_ n. see "Regional Dishes" p. 51

γουρουνοπουλο στο φουρνο _goo-roo-noh-poo-loh stoh foor-noh_ n. pork (baked)

γουστο _goos-toh_ n. taste

γραμμα _grah-mah_ n. letter

γραμματοκιβωτιο _grah-mah-toh-kee-voh-tee-oh_ n. letter-box

γραμματοσημο _grah-mah-tos-see-moh_ n. postage stamp

γραμμη _grah-mee_ f. line

γρανιτα _grah-nee-tah_ f. shaved ice

γρατσουνια _grat-tsoo-nee-ah_ f. scratch

γραφη _grah-fee_ f. writing

γραφω _grah-foh_ f. write, to

γριππη _gree-pee_ f. flu

γυαλι _yah-lee_ n. glass

γυαλια _yah-lee-ah_ pl. spectacles

γυμναζω _yim-nah-zoh_ v. to exercise

γυμναστικη _yim-nahs-tee-kee_ f. gymnastics

γυμνος _yeem-nohs_ adj. nude

γυναικα *yee-neh-kah* f. woman, wife

γυναικολογος *yee-neh-koh-loh-gos* m. gynaecologist

γυρος *yee-ros* m. roasting-spit

γωνια *goh-nee-ah* f. corner

δαγκωνω *dah-goh-noh* v. to bite

δαμασκηνο *dah-mahs-kee-noh* n. plum

δανειζω *dah-nee-zoh* v. to lend

δαπανη *dah-pah-nee* f. purchase

δασκαλος *dahs-kah-los* m. teacher (man) δασκαλα *dahs-kah-lah* f. teacher (woman)

δασμος *dahs-mos* m. tax, levy

δασος *dahs-sos* n. forest δασοφυλακας *dahs-soh-fee-lah-kas* m. forest warden

δαφνη *dahf-nee* n. bay (leaf)

δαχτυλιδι *dah-tee-lee-dee* n. ring

δαχτυλο *dah-tee-loh* n. finger

δειγμα *deeg-mah* n. sample

δειπνιζω *dip-nee-zoh* v. to have supper

δειπνο *deep-noh* n. supper

δειχνω *deeh-noh* v. to show

δεκαδα *deh-kah-dah* f. (about) ten

δεκαρικο *deh-kah-ree-koh* n. 10-drachma coin

Δεκεμβριος *deh-kem-vree-ohs* m. December

δεμα *deh-mah* n. parcel

Δεμεστιχα *deh-mes-tee-hah* see "Wines" p. 25

δεν *den* adv. not

δεντρο *den-droh* n. tree

δεντρολιβανο *den-droh-lee-vah-noh* n. rosemary

δεξιωση *deh-xee-ohs-see* f. reception

δερματολογος *der-mah-toh-loh-gos* m. dermatologist

δεσποινιδα *des-pee-nee-dah* f. Miss, young lady

δευτερος *def-teh-ros* adj. second

δεχομαι *deh-hoh-meh* v. to receive, to accept

δηλαδη *dee-lah-dee* conj. that is, or rather

δηλητηριο *dee-lee-tee-ree-oh* n. poison

δηλωνω *dee-loh-noh* v. to declare

δημητριακα *dee-mee-tree-ah-kah* n. pl. cereals

δημοκρατια *dee-moh-krah-tee-ah* f. democracy

δημος _dee-mos_ m. city hall

δημοσιογραφια _dee-mohs-see-oh-grah-fee-ah_ f. journalism

δημοσιος _dee-mohs-see-os_ adj. public

διαβαζω _dee-ah-vah-zoh_, to read

διαβατηριο _dee-ah-vah-tee-ree-oh_ n. passport

διαιρω _dee-eh-roh_ v. to divide

διαιτα _dee-eh-tah_ f. diet

διακοπες, _dee-ah-koh-pes_ pl. vacations

διακοπη _dee-ah-koh-pee_ f. interruption

διακοπτης _dee-ah-kop-tis_ m. switch

διαλεγω _dee-ah-leh-goh_ v. to choose

διαλογος _dee-ah-loh-gos_ m. dialogue

διαμαρτυρομαι _dee-ah-mar-tee-roh-meh_ v. to protest

διαμερισμα _dee-ah-meh-rees-mah_ n. apartment

διαμονη _dee-ah-moh-nee_ f. residence

διανοια _dee-ah-nee-ah_ f. intellect

διαπλους _dee-ah-ploos_ m. navigation

διαρκεια _dee-ar-kee-yah_ d. duration

διαρροια _dee-ar-ee-ah_ f. diarrhea

διασκεδαζω _dee-ahs-keh-dah-zoh_ v. amuse oneself, to

διασταυρωση _dee-ah-stav-ros-see_ f. crossroad

διασωζω _dee-ah-so-zoh_ v. to save

διατηρω _dee-ah-tee-roh_ v. to keep

διατροφη _dee-ah-troh-fee_ f. food

διαφημιση _dee-ah-fee-mis-see_ f. advertisement

διαφορα _dee-ah-for-ah_ f. difference

διαφωνια _dee-ah-foh-nee-ah_ f. contrast

διδασκω _dee-dahs-koh_ v. to teach

διεθνης _dee-eth-nees_ adj. international

διερμηνεας _dee-er-mee-neh-ahs_ m. interpreter

διευθυνση _dee-ef-thin-see_ f. direction, address

διευθυνση γραμματος _dee-ef-thin-see grah-mah-tos_ f. mailing address

διευκολυνση _dee-ef-koh-lin-see_ f. facility

δινω _dee-noh_ v. give, to

διοδιο _dee-oh-dee-oh_ n. toll

διπλος _dip-los_ adj. double

δισκοθηκη _dis-koh-thee-kee_ f. discothèque

διχτυ _deeh-tee_ n. net

διχως _dee-hos_ adv. without

διψα _deep-sah_ f. thirst

δοκιμαζω _doh-kee-ma-zoh_ v. to try, to taste

δολωμα _doh-loh-mah_ n. bait

δοντι _don-dee_ n. tooth

δραχμη _drah-mee_ f. drachma

δρομος _droh-mos_ m. street

δυοσμος _dee-os-mos_ m. mint

δυσαρεσκεια _dis-sah-res-kee-ah_ f. disappointment

Δυση _dees-see_ f. sunset

δυσκολια _dis-koh-lee-ah_ f. difficulty

δυσπεψια _dis-pep-see-ah_ f. indigestion

δωδεκαδα _doh-deh-kah-dah_ f. dozen

δωματιο _doh-mah-ee-oh_ n. room

δωρεαν _doh-reh-ahn_ adv. for free

δωρο _doh-roh_ n. gift

εαν _eh-ahn_ conj. if

εβδομαδα _ev-doh-mah-dah_ f. week

εγγυηση _eh-gee-ees-see_ f. warranty

εγγυουμαι _eh-ghee-oo-meh_ v. guarantee, to

εγκαυμα _eh-ghav-mah_ n. burn

εγω _eh-goh_ pron. I

εδαφος _eh-dah-fos_ n. ground

εδω _eh-doh_ adv. here

εθνικοτητα _eth-nee-koh-tee-tah_ f. nationality

εθνος _eth-nos_ n. nation

ειδηση _ee-dis-see_ f. news

ειδοπιω _ee-doh-pee-oh_ v. to warn

εικονα _ee-koh-nah_ f. picture

ειμαι _ee-meh_ v. be, to πως εισθε _pohs is-theh_ how are you?

ειρηνη _ee-ree-nee_ f. peace

εισιτηριο _iss-see-tee-ree-oh_ n. ticket

εισοδος _ees-soh-dos_ f. entrance

Εκαλη _eh-kah-lee_ see "Wines" p. 25

εκατονταδα _eh-kah-ton-dah-dah_ f. a hundred

εκατοσταρικο _eh-kah-toh-stah-ree-koh_ n. 100-drachma coin

εκδρομη _ek-droh-mee_ f. excursion

εκει _eh-kee_ adv. there

εκεινος _eh-kee-nos_ m. that

εκλογη *ek-loh-yee* f. choice

εκπτωση *ek-ptos-see* f. discount

εκφραζω *ek-frah-zoh* v. to express

ελα, ελατε *eh-lah, eh-lah-teh* v. Come! sing., pl.

ελαιολαδο *el-eh-oh-lah-doh* n. olive oil

ελαττωματικος *el-lah-toh-mah-tee-kos* adj. faulty

ελαφρος *eh-lah-fros* adj. light (weight)

Ελβετος *el-veh-tos* m. Swiss (man)

ελευθερια *el-ef-theh-ree-ah* f. freedom

ελια *eh-lee-ah* f. olive

Ελληνας *el-lee-nahs* m. Greek (man)

Ελληνιδα *el-lee-nee-dah* f. Greek (woman)

ελληνικα *el-lee-nee-kah* n. Greek language

ελπιδα *el-pee-dah* f. hope

εμεις *eh-mees* pro. we

εμμηνα *eh-mee-nah* n. pl. menstruation

εμπιστοσυνη *eh-bis-toss-see-nee* f. trust

εμποριο *em-boh-ree-oh* n. trade

εμπρος *em-bros* adv. come in, ready

ενδυμα *en-dee-mah* n. dress

ενεση *eh-ness-see* f. injection

ενηλικος *eh-nee-lee-kos* adj. of age

ενθυμια *en-thee-mee-ah* n. pl. souvenir

ενθυμιζω *en-thee-mee-zoh* v. to remember

εννοια *eh-nee-ah* f. sense, direction

εννοω *eh-noh-oh* v. to mean

ενοικιαζω *eh-nee-kee-ah-zoh* v. to rent

ενοχληση *eh-noh-lis-see* f. disturbance

ενσημο *en-see-moh* n. revenue stamp

εν ταξει *en tahk-see* adv. it's fine

εντελως *en-deh-los* adv. completely

εντερο *en-deh-roh* n. intestine

εντομοκτονο *en-doh-mok-toh-noh* n. insecticide

εντονος *en-doh-nos* adj. intense

εντυπωση *en-dee-pos-see* f. impression

ενω *eh-noh* conj. while

ενωνω *en-noh-noh* v. to unite

εξαγω *ex-ah-goh* v. to export

εξηγηση *ex-ee-yee-see* f. explanation

εξοδο *ex-oh-doh* n. expense, purchase

εξοδος *ex-oh-dos* f. exit

εξοφληση *ex-oh-flis-see* f. balance of account

εξοφλω *ex-oh-floh* v. to settle (an account)

εξοχη *ex-oh-hee* f. campaign, country

εξοχοτητα *ex-oh-hoh-tee-tah* f. excellence

εξω *ex-oh* adv. outside

εξωτερικος *ex-oh-teh-ree-kos* adj. external

εορτη *eh-or-tee* f. party

επαγγελμα *eh-pah-ghel-mah* n. profession

επαναλαβαινω *eh-pah-nah-lah-veh-noh* v. to repeat

επανω *eh-pah-noh* adv. above, up

επαρχια *eh-par-hee-ah* f. province

επειγων *eh-pee-gon* adj. urgent

επειδη *eh-pee-dee* conj. since

επετειος *eh-peh-tee-os* f. anniversary

επιβατης *eh-pee-vah-tis* m. passenger

επιβιβαση *eh-pee-vee-vahs-see* f. embarkation

επιγραφη *eh-pee-grah-fee* f. signboard

επιδεσμος *eh-pee-des-mos* m. bandage

επιδορπιο *eh-pee-dor-pee-oh* n. dessert

επικαιρος *eh-pee-keh-ros* adj. present

επικινδυνος *eh-pee-keen-dee-nos* adj. dangerous

επισης *eh-peess-sis* adv. likewise

επισκεπτομαι *eh-pis-kep-toh-meh* v. to visit

επισκευαζω *eh-pis-keh-vah-zoh* v. repair, to

επισκεψη *eh-pis-kep-see* f. visit

επιστολοχαρτο *eh-pis-toh-loh-har-toh* n. writing-paper

επιστρεφω *eh-pis-treh-foh* v. return, to

επιταγη *eh-pee-tah-yee* f. check

επιτρεπω *eh-pee-treh-poh* v. to permit

εποχη *eh-poh-hee* f. season

επωνημο *eh-poh-nee-moh* n. surname

εργαζομαι *er-gah-zoh-meh* v; to work

εργασιμος *er-gas-see-mohs* adj. workday

ερχομαι *er-hoh-meh* v. to come

ερωτω *eh-roh-toh* v. to ask

εσεις eh-<u>sees</u> pron. you (pl.)

εσυ es-<u>see</u> you (sing.)

εστιατοριο es-tee-ah-<u>toh</u>-ree-oh n. restaurant

ετσι <u>et</u>-see adv. thus, like this

ευγενικος ev-gheh-nee-<u>kos</u> adj. nice

Ευρωπαιος ev-roh-<u>peh</u>-os adj. European

ευχαριστω ef-hah-ris-<u>toh</u> v. to thank

εφημεριδα eh-fee-meh-<u>ree</u>-dah f. newspaper

εχω <u>eh</u>-hoh v. to have

ζαμπον zam-<u>bon</u> n. baked ham

ζαρκαδι zar-<u>kah</u>-dee n. roebuck

ζαχαρη <u>zah</u>-hah-ree f. sugar

ζαχαριερα zah-hah-ree-<u>eh</u>-rah f. sugarbowl

ζαχαροπλαστειο zah-hah-roh-plahs-<u>tee</u>-oh n. pastry shop

ζαχαροπλαστις zah-hah-roh-<u>plas</u>-tis m. confectioner

ζαχαροπουλια Λεσβου zah-hah-roh-<u>poo</u>-lee-ah <u>lev</u>-soo see "Recipes" p. 69

ζαχαροτευτλο zah-hah-<u>roh</u>-tef-loh n. beetroot

ζαχαρωνω zah-hah-<u>roh</u>-noh v. to sweeten

ζελατινη zeh-lah-<u>tee</u>-nee f. jelly

ζελε γλυκα zeh-<u>leh</u> glee-<u>kah</u> pl. jello desserts

ζεσταινω zes-<u>teh</u>-noh v. warm, to

ζεστος zeh-<u>stohs</u> adj. hot

ζεστη <u>zeh</u>-stee f. heat

ζητηση <u>zee</u>-tis-see f. request

ζητω zee-<u>toh</u> v. to ask, to seek

ζουμι zoo-<u>mee</u> n. broth

ζυγαρια zee-gah-ree-<u>ah</u> f. scales

ζυμαρι zee-<u>mah</u>-ree f. paste, pasta

ζυμαρικα zee-mah-ree-<u>kah</u> pl. starchy foods

ζυμη <u>zee</u>-mee f. paste, dough

ζω <u>zoh</u> v. to live

ζωη zoh-<u>ee</u> f. life

ζωμος zoh-<u>mos</u> m. sauce

ζωο zoh-oh n. animal

Η, η ee art. f. the

ηδη <u>ee</u>-dee adv. already

ηλιος <u>ee</u>-lee-os m. sun

ηλιοτροπιο ee-lee-oh-<u>troh</u>-pee-oh n. sunflower

ημερα ee-<u>meh</u>-rah f. day

ημερολογιο ee-meh-roh-<u>loh</u>-yee-oh n. calendar

ημερομηνια ee-meh-roh-mee-<u>nee</u>-ah f. date

ημισυ *ee-miss-ee* n. half

ΗΠΑ *ee-pah* USA

ηρεμιστικο *ee-reh-mis-tee-koh* n. sedative

ησυχια *is-see-hee-ah* f. quiet, silence

ηχος *ee-hos* m. sound

ηχω *ee-hoh* f. echo

θα *thah* part. to conjugate the future tense

θαλαμηγος *thah-lah-mee-gos* f. sailing-boat

θαλασσινα *thah-lahs-see-nah* pl. seafood

θαλασσινα βραστα *thah-lahs-see-nah vras-tah*, boiled seafood, see "National Dishes" p. 34

θαλασσινα τηγανητα *thah-lahs-see-nah tee-gah-nee-tah* fried seafood, see "National Dishes" p. 34

θαλασσινα ωμα *thah-lahs-see-nah oh-mah* raw seafood, see "National Dishes" p. 34

θελω *theh-loh* v. to want,

Θεος *theh-os* m. God

θερμιδα *ther-mee-dah* f. calorie

θερμοκρασια *ther-moh-kras-see-ah* f. temperature

θερμοσιφωνας *ther-moh-see-foh-nas* f. waterheater

Θεσσαλια *thes-sah-lee-ah* Thessalia

θρεπτικος *threp-tee-kos* adj. nourishing

θυρωρος *thee-roh-ros* m. porter

Ιανουαριος *ee-ah-noo-ah-ree-os* m. January

ιατρειο *ee-ah-tree-oh* n. doctor's office, out-patients clinic

ιατρος *ee-ah-tros* m. doctor

Ιησους *ee-ee-soos* m. Jesus

ιθαγενεια *ee-thah-geh-nee-ah* f. citizenship

ικανοποιω *ee-kah-noh-pee-oh* v. to satisfy

Ιουλιος *ee-oo-lee-os* m. July

Ιουνιος *ee-oo-nee-os* m. June

ιππος *ee-pos* m. horse

ισιος *ees-see-os* adj. straight

ισκιος *ees-kee-os* m. shade

ισος *ees-sos* adj. equal

Ισπανος *is-pah-nos* m. Spanish

ιταλικα *ee-tah-lee-kah* pl. Italian (language)

Ιταλος *ee-tah-los* Italian

ιχθυοπωλειο *eek-thee-oh-poh-lee-oh* fishmarket

Καβα Καμπα *kah-vah kam-bah* see "Wines" p. 25

καβουρας *kah-voo-ras* m. crab

καθαριζω *kah-thah-ree-zoh* v. clean, to

καθε *kah-theh* pr. every, each

καθισμα *kah-this-mah* n. seat

και *keh* conj. and

καιμακι *kah-ee-mah-kee* n. fresh cream see "Sweets" p. 22

καιρος *keh-ros* m. weather

κακαβια *kah-kah-vee-ah* see "National Dishes" p. 34

κακαο *kah-kah-oh* cocoa

κακος *kah-kos* adj. bad

καλαμακι *kah-lah-mah-kee* n. straw

καλαμαρακια γεμιστα *kah-lah-mah-rah-kee-ah yeh-mis-tah* stuffed squid, see "National Dishes" p. 35

καλαμαρακια κρασατα *kah-lah-mah-rah-kee-ah kras-sah-tah* squid cooked in wine see "National Dishes" p. 35

καλαμαρακια τηγανητα *kah-lah-mah-rah-kee-ah tee-gah-nee-tah* fried squid, see "National Dishes" p. 35

καλαμαρακια στο φουρνο *kah-lah-mah-rah-kee-ah stoh foor-no* baked squid see "Regional Dishes" p. 52

καλαμαρι *kah-lah-mah-ree* n. squid

καλημερα *kah-lee-meh-rah* f. good morning

καληνυκτα *kah-lee-neek-tah* f. good night

καλησπερα *kah-lis-peh-rah* f. good evening

καλοκαιρι *kah-loh-keh-ree* n. summer

καλος, καλα *kah-los, kah-lah* adj. good, well

καλοψημενος *kah-lop-see-meh-nos* adj. well-done

καλτσουνια *kalt-soo-nee-ah* see "Regional Dishes" p. 53

κανω *kah-noh* v. to do, to make

καπαρο *kah-pah-roh* n. deposit

καπνισμα *kap-nis-mah* n. smoking

καπνιστος *kap-nis-tos* adj. smoked

καραμελα *kah-rah-meh-lah* caramel, candy κρεμ καραμελ *Krem kah-rah-mel* flan

καρβουνο *kar-voo-noh* n. coal στα καρβουνα *stah kar-voo-na* barbecued

καρδια *kar-dee-ah* f. heart

καροτο *kah-roh-toh* n.
carrot

καρπος *kar-pos* n. m. fruit

καρπουζι *kar-poo-zee* n.
watermelon

καρυδι *kah-ree-dee* n. nut,
see also "Liqueurs" p. 27

καρυκευμα *kah-ree-kev-mah*
n. spice

κασερι *kahs-seh-ree* n. see
"Cheeses" p. 17

κασερι πεϊνιρλι *kahs-seh-ree
peh-ee-nir-lee* see "Regional
Dishes" p. 46

καστανο *kahs-tah-noh* n.
chestnut

καστανου (παστα) *kahs-tah-
noo* pasta with chestnuts

καταιφι *kah-tah-ee-fee* see
"Sweets" p. 21

καταλογος *kah-tah-loh-gos*
m. list, καταλογος φαγητων
*kah-tah-loh-gos fah-ghee-
ton* m. menu

καταστημα *kah-tas-tee-mah*
n. store

κατοικια *kah-tee-kee-ah* f.
residence

καττσαρολα *kaht-sah-roh-
lah* f. stew

καφενειο *kah-feh-nee-oh* n.
coffee-house

καφες *kah-fes* coffee
ελληνικος *eh-lee-nee-kos*

Greek coffee, με γαλα *meh
gah-lah* coffee with milk

κεντρο *ken-droh* n.
downtown

κερασι *keh-rahs-see* n.
cherry

κεφαλογρουβιερα *keh-fah-
loh-groo-vee-eh-rah* see
"Cheeses" p. 17

κεφαλοτυρι *keh-fah-loh-tee-
ree* see "Cheeses" p. 17

κεφτεδες *kef-teh-des*
meatballs, see "National
Dishes" p. 35

Κισσαμος *kees-sah-mos* see
"Wines" p. 25

κηπος *kee-pos* m. garden

κιλο *kee-loh* n. kilo

κλιμα *klee-mah* n. climate

κλιματισμος *klee-mah-tis-
mos* air-conditioned

Κνωσσος *knos-sos* see
"Wines" p. 25

κοκορετσι *koh-koh-ret-see*
see "National Dishes" p. 35

κοκορετσι Καρδιτσας *koh-
koh-ret-see kar-deet-sas* see
"Regional Dishes" p. 47

κολοκυθακια γεμιστα *koh-
loh-kee-thah-kee-ah yeh-
mis-tah* stuffed zucchini

κολοκυθακια τηγανιτα *koh-
loh-kee-thah-kee-ah tee-
gah-nee-tah* fried zucchini

κοκκινογουλι *koh-kee-noh-goo-lee* n. beetroot

κοκτειλ *kok-teyl* cocktail

κολατσιο πρωινο *koh-laht-tsee-oh/proh-ee-noh* breakfast

κολοκυθα *koh-loh-kee-thah* f. pumpkin

κονιακ *koh-nee-ak* cognac

κοσμημα *kos-mee-mah* n. jewel

κοσμος *kos-mos* m. world, people

κοτα *koh-tah* f. hen

κοτολετες αρνι με σαλτσα *koh-toh-leh-tes ahr-nee meh sahl-tsah* see "National Dishes" p. 35

κοτολετες αρνισιες *koh-toh-leh-tes ahr-nees-see-es* pl. cutlets (lamb)

κοτολετες χοιρινες *koh-toh-leh-tes hee-ree-nes* pl. cutlets (pork)

κοτοπιτα Κριτης *koh-toh-pee-tah kree-tis* chicken country pie see "Regional Dishes" p. 49

κοτοπουλο *koh-toh-poo-loh* n. chicken, γυρου *yee-roo* on the spit, ψητο *psee-toh* roasted, στα *stah kahr-voo-nah* barbecued

κοτοπουλο λεμονατο *koh-toh-poo-loh leh-moh-nah-toh* chicken with lemon, see "National Dishes" p. 36

κοτοπουλο με μπαμιες *koh-toh-poo-loh meh bah-mee-es* chicken with okra see "National Dishes" p. 36

κοτοπουλο με χυλοπιτες *koh-toh-poo-loh meh hee-loh-pee-tes* chicken and tagliatelle, see "National Dishes" p. 36

κουβερ *koo-ver* cover, lid

κουζινα *koo-zee-nah* f. kitchen

κουλουρακια *koo-loo-rah-kyah* pl. biscuits see "Other Specialties" p. 29

κουνελι *koo-neh-lee* n. rabbit κουνελι στιφαδο *koo-neh-lee stee-fah-doh* stewed rabbit

κουκια με γιαουρτι *koo-kyah meh yah-oor-tee* broad beans with yoghurt see "Regional Dishes" p. 48

κουκια φρεσκα *koo-kyah fres-kah* green broad beans, see "National Dishes" p. 36

κουνουπιδι *koo-noo-pee-dee* n. cauliflower

κουραμπιεδες *koo-rah-bee-eh-des* see "Sweet" p. 22

Κουρος _koo-ros_ see "Wines"
p. 25

Κουρτακι _koor-tah-kee_ see
"Wines" p. 25

κουταλι _koo-tah-lee_ n.
tablespoon

κουτι _koo-tee_ n. box

κουφετο _koo-feh-toh_ n.
sugar-coated almonds

κρασι _krahs-see_ n. wine

κρεας _kreh_-ahs n. meat,

κυμα _kee-mah_ minced meat

κρεας αρνι κοκκινιστο _kreh_-
ahs ahr-_nee_ koh-kee-nis-_toh_
see "Regional Dishes" p. 47

κρεας κοκκινιστο _kreh_-ahs
koh-kee-nis-_toh_ _meat_ with
tomato, see "National
Dishes" p. 36

κρεατοπιτα _kreh-ah-toh-pee-_
tah meat country pie see
"Regional Dishes" p. 49

κρεατοπιτα κεφαλονιτικη
kreh-ah-toh-pee-tah keh-
fah-loh-nee-tee-kee see
"Regional Dishes" p. 57

κρεατοπιτα κρητης _kreh-ah-_
toh-pee-tah kree-tis see
"Regional Dishes" p. 53

κρεμμυδι _kreh-mee-dee_ n.
onion

κρεμυδοπιτα _kreh-mee-doh-_
pee-tah onion country pie
see "Regional Dishes" p. 55

κριαρι _kree-ah-ree_ n. mutton

κριθαρι _kree-thah-ree_ n.
barley

κρυος _kree-os_ adj. cold

κταποδια _ktah-poh-dyah_
polyps

κυβος _kee-vos_ m. cube,

κυδωνια με κρεας, _kee-doh-_
nee-ah meh kreh-ahs
quince with meat, see
"National Dishes" p. 36

κυνηγι _kee-nee-yee_ n.
hunting

κωπηλατω _koh-pee-lah-toh_
v. to row

λαγος _lah-gos_ m. hare

λαγος στιφαδο _lah-gos_
stee-fah-doh stewed hare,
see "National Dishes"
p. 36

λαδερα γιαχνι _lah-deh-rah_
yah-nee see "Regional
Dishes" p. 46

λαδι _lah-dee_ n. oil

λαδικο _lah-dee-koh_ n. oil
cruet

λαδοκολα _lah-doh-koh-lah_
n. wrapped and steamed
dishes

λαδολεμονο _lah-doh-leh-_
moh-noh n. dressings for
salads based on oil and
lemon

λαιμαργος *leh-mar-gos* adj. gourmand

λακερδα *lah-ker-dah* f. see "National Dishes" p. 36

λαχανικα *lah-hah-nee-kah* pl. vegetables

λαχανο *lah-hah-noh* n. cabbage

λαχανοντολμαδες *lah-hah-noh-dol-mah-des* pl. rolls with Savoy cabbage

λαχανοπιτα *lah-hah-noh-pee-tah* see "Regional Dishes" p. 55

λεγω *leh-goh* v. to say

λεμοναδα *leh-moh-nah-dah*, lemonade

λεμονι *leh-moh-nee* n. lemon see also "Liqueurs" p. 27

λεξικο *lex-ee-koh* n. dictionary

λεωφορειο *leh-oh-foh-ree-oh* n. bus

λεωφορος *leh-oh-foh-ros* f. street

λιγος *lee-gos* adj. little

λιπος *lee-pos* n. grease, fat

λιτρο *lee-troh* n. liter

λιχουδιες *lee-hoo-dee-es* pl. sweets

λογαριασμος *loh-gah-ree-ahs-mos* m. bill

λοιπον *lee-pon* therefore

λουκανικο *loo-kah-nee-koh* n. sausage see "Sausages and Cold Cuts" p. 15

λουκουμια *loo-koo-mee-ah* pl. see "Sweets" p. 22

μα *mah* conj. but

μαγειρας *mah-yee-rahs* m. cook

μαγειρευω *mah-yee-reh-voh* v, to cook

μαγια *mah-yah* f. brewer's yeast

μαγιονεζα *mah-yoh-ne-zah* f. mayonnaise

μαζι *mah-zee* conj. together

μαιντανος *mah-in-dah-nos* m. parsley

Μαιος *mah-ee-os* m. May

μακαροναδα *mah-kah-roh-nah-dah* f. pasta with sauce see "National Dishes" p. 37

μακαρονια *mah-kah-roh-nyah* pl. macaroni

μακαρονια με κρεας *mah-kah-roh-nyah meh kreh-ahs* see "National Dishes" p. 37

μακαρονια με κυμα *mah-kah-roh-nyah meh kee-mah* see "National Dishes" p. 37

μακαρονια παστιτσιο *mah-kah-roh-nyah pahs-steet-see-oh* see "National Dishes" p. 37

μακαρονια φουρνου *mah-*

kah-<u>roh</u>-nyah <u>foor</u>-noo see
"Regional Dishes" p. 54

μαλιστα *mah-lis-tah* adv.
yes, certainly

μανιταρι *mah-nee-<u>tah</u>-ree* n.
tangerine

μανουρι *mah-<u>noo</u>-ree* see
"Cheeses" p. 17

μανταρινι *mahn-dah-<u>ree</u>-nee*
n. manderin

Μαντινια *mahn-tee-<u>nee</u>-ah*
see "Wines" p. 25

μαξιλαρι *mahx-ee-<u>lah</u>-ree* n.
cushion, pillow

μαραθο *<u>mah</u>-rah-thoh* n.
fennel

μαργαρινη *mar-gah-<u>ree</u>-nee*
f. margarine

μαριδες *mah-<u>ree</u>-des* pl.
smelts

μαριδες τηγανητες *mah-<u>ree</u>-des tee-gah-nee-<u>tes</u>* see
"National Dishes" p. 37 and
"Regional Dishes" p. 52

μαρμελαδα *mar-meh-<u>lah</u>-dah* f. jam

μαρουλι *mah-<u>roo</u>-lee* n.
lettuce

Μαρτιος *<u>mar</u>-tee-os* m.
March

μαστιχα *mahs-<u>tee</u>-ha* mastic,
see "Liqueurs" p. 27

μαστιχα γλυκο *mahs-<u>tee</u>-hah glee-<u>koh</u>* see

"Regional Dishes" p. 56

ματι *<u>mah</u>-tee* n. eye

Μαυροδαφνη *mahv-roh-<u>dahf</u>-nee* see "Wines" p. 25

μαχαιρι *mah-<u>heh</u>-ree* n.
knife

μαχαιροπιρουνα *mah-heh-roh-<u>pee</u>-roo-nah* pl. cutlery

Μαχλεπι *mah-<u>leh</u>-pee* see
"Other Specialties" p. 30

με *meh* conj. with

μεζες *meh-<u>zes</u>* m. hors-
d'oeuvre, μεζεδες *meh-<u>zeh</u>-des* pl. appetizers,
μεζεδακια n. pl. *meh-zeh-<u>dah</u>-kyah* bite-size
appetizers

μεζεδοπωλειο *meh-zeh-doh-poh-<u>lee</u>-oh* n. a place where
appetizers are served

μελι *<u>meh</u>-lee* n. honey, see
"Sweets" p. 22

μελισσα *<u>meh</u>-lis-sah* f. bee

μελιτζανα *meh-lee-<u>zah</u>-nah*
f. eggplant

μελιτζανακι *meh-lee-zah-<u>nah</u>-kee* see "Regional
Dishes" p. 56

μελιτζανες γεμιστες *meh-lee-<u>zah</u>-nes yeh-mis-<u>tes</u>* see
"National Dishes" p. 37

μελιτζανες γιαχνι *meh-lee-<u>zah</u>-nes yah-<u>nee</u>* eggplant
with sauce

μελιτζανες παπουτσακια *meh-lee-zah-nes pah-poot-sah-kyah* see "National Dishes" p. 37

μελιτζανες τηγανητες *meh-lee-zah-nes tee-gah-nee-tes* see "National Dishes" p. 37

μελιτζανες τουρσι *meh-lee-zah-nes toor-see* pickled eggplants

μελιτζανοσαλατα *meh-lee-zah-noh-sah-lah-tah* see "Sauces and Condiments" p. 19 and "Recipes" p. 62

μελομακαρονα *meh-loh-mah-kah-roh-nah* see "Sweets" p. 22

μεντα *men-tah* f. mint

μεριδα *meh-ree-dah* f. portion

μεσανυχτα *mes-sah-nik-tah* n. midnight

μεσημερι *mehs-see-meh-ree* n. noon

μετα *meh-tah* adv. later, after

Μεταξα *meh-tahx-sah* see "Liqueurs" p. 27

μηλο *mee-loh* n. apple

μηλοπιτα *mee-loh-pee-tah* f. apple strudel

μηνας *mee-nahs* m. month

μιγμα *meeg-mah* n. mix

μιλω *mee-loh* v. to speak

μορταδελλα *mor-tah-del-lah* see "Sausages and Cold Cuts", p. 15

μοσχαρι *mos-hah-ree* n. veal

μοσχαρι κρασατο *mos-kah-ree kras-sah-toh* see "National Dishes" p. 38

Μοσχατο *mos-hah-toh* see "Wines" p. 25

μουσακας ζαρζαβατικα *moos-sah-kas zar-zah-vah-tee-kah* see "National Dishes" p. 38

μουσακας μελιτζανες *moos-sah-kas meh-lee-zah-nes* see "National Dishes" p. 38 and "Recipes" p. 63

μουσταλευρια *moos-tah-lehv-ree-ah* see "Sweets" p. 23

μπακαλιαρακια τηγανητα *bah-kah-lee-ah-rah-kyah tee-gah-nee-tah* see "National Dishes" p. 38

μπακαλιαρος *bah-kah-lee-ah-ros* m. dried cod

μπακαλιαρος γιαχνι *bah-kah-lee-ah-ros yah-nee* see "National Dishes" p. 38

μπακαλιαρος σκορδαλια *bah-kah-lee-ah-ros skor-dah-lee-ah* see "Regional Dishes" p. 46

μπακλαβας *bak-lah-vahs* see "Sweets" p. 23

μπαμιες _bah-mee-es_ see
"Other Specialties" p. 30

μπαμιες γιαχνι _bah-mee-es
yah-nee_ see "National
Dishes" p. 38

μπαμιες με κοτοπουλο _bah-
mee-es meh koh-toh-poo-
loh_ okra with chicken see
"National Dishes" p. 38

μπαμιες με κρεας _bah-mee-
es meh kreh-ahs_ see
"National Dishes" p. 38

μπανανα _bah-nah-nah_ f.
banana

μπαρ _bar_ n. café

μπαρμπουνια _bar-boo-nyah_
pl. mullets

μπεκατσα κρασατη _beh-kah-
tsah krahs-sah-tee_
woodcock in wine see
"Regional Dishes" p. 57

μπεσαμελλα αλλα ελληνικα
_beh-shah-mel-lah ahl-lah el-
leeh-nee-kah_ see "Sauces
and Condiments" p. 19

μπιρα _bee-rah_ f. beer

μπιραρια _bee-rah-ree-ah_ f.
inn, beer-house

μπισκοτο _bis-koh-toh_ n.
biscuit

μπιφτεκια σκαρας _bif-teh-
kyah skah-rahs_ see
"National Dishes" p. 38

μπομποτα με μπριζολες

χοιρινες _boh-boh-tah
meh bri-zoh-les hee-
ree-nes_ see "Regional
Dishes" p. 44

μπορω _boh-roh_ v. to be able
to

μποτιλια _boh-tee-lyah_ f.
bottle

μπουγατσα Θεσσαλονικης
_boo-gaht-tsah thes-sah-loh-
nee-kis_ see "Regional
Dishes" p. 46

μπουκαλι _boo-kah-lee_ n.
bottle

μπουρδετο _boor-deh-toh_ see
"Regional Dishes" p. 58

μπουρεκακια _boo-reh-kah-
kyah_ see "National Dishes"
p. 38

μπουρεκια με χαλουμι _boo-
reh-kyah meh hah-loo-mee_
see "Regional Dishes" p. 52

μπουτι _boo-tee_ n. leg,
χοιρινο _hee-ree-noh_, leg of
pork, μοσχαρισιο _mos-
khah-rees-see-oh_ of veal

μπριζολα _bree-zoh-lah_ f.
steak

μπριζολα μοσχαρισια _bree-
zoh-lah mos-khah-rees-sah_
f. veal steak

μπριζολα χοιρινη _brit-zoh-
lah hee-ree-nee_ f. pork
chop

μυαλο *mee-ah-loh* n. brain, βραστα πανε *vrahs-tah pah-neh* breaded boiled brain

μυδια *mee-dee-ah* pl. mussels

μυρωδια *mee-roh-dee-ah* f. smell

Μυστρα *miss-trah* see "Liqueurs" p. 26

Μυστρα Ουζο *miss-trah oo-zoh* see "Liqueurs" p. 27

Μυτζηθρα *mee-zee-thrah* see "Cheeses" p. 18

μυτη *mee-tee* f. nose

μωλος *moh-los* m. quay

να *nah* conj. that, here is

ναι *neh* adv. yes

νερο *neh-roh* n. water

Νεστωρ *nes-tor* see "Wines" p. 26

νησι *nis-see* n. island

Νοεμβριος *noh-em-vree-os* m. November

νομιζω *noh-mee-zoh* v. to believe

νομισμα *noh-mis-mah* n. coin

νοσοκομειο *nos-soh-koh-mee-oh* n. hospital

νοστιμαδα *nos-tee-mah-dah* f. taste

Νοτος *noh-tos* m. South

ντολμαδακια *dol-mah-dah-kyah* see "National Dishes" p. 39

ντολμαδακια με κυμα *dol-mah-dah-kyah meh kee-mah* see "National Dishes" p. 39

ντολμαδες *dohl-mah-des* see "National Dishes" p. 39

ντοματα *doh-mah-ta* f. tomato

ντοματες γεμιστες *doh-mah-tes yeh-mis-tes* stuffed tomatoes see "National Dishes" p. 39

ντοματες με αυγα *doh-mah-tes meh av-gah* see "National Dishes" p. 39

ντοματοσαλατα *doh-mah-toh-sah-lah-tah* tomato salad see "National Dishes" p. 39

νυχτα *neeh-tah* f. night

νωπα κρεατα *noh-pah kreh-ah-tah,* fresh meat

νωπος *noh-pos* m. fresh

ξανα *ksah-nah* adv. again

ξανα *ksah-nah* prefix re-

ξενοδοχειο *kseh-noh-doh-hee-oh* n. hotel

ξενος *kseh-nos* m. foreigner

ξερος *kseh-ros* adj. dry

ξερω *kseh-roh* v. to know

ξεχνω *kseh-noh* v. to forget

ξιδι *ksee-dee* n. vinegar

ξινογλυκος *ksee-noh-glee-kos* adj. sweet-and-sour

ξινος *ksee-nos* adj. sour

ξιφιας *ksee-fee-ahs* m.
 swordfish
ξιφιας σκαρας *ksee-fee-ahs
 skah-rahs* see "National
 Dishes" p. 39
ξιφιας σουβλακι *ksee-fee-
 ahs soov-lah-kee* see
 "National Dishes" p. 39
ξυπνητηρι *ksip-nee-tee-ree*
 n. alarm clock
ξυπνω *ksip-noh* v. to awaken

Ο, οι *oh, ee* art. the, pl. the
οδηγω *oh-dee-goh* v. to drive
οδοντογλυφιδα *oh-don-
 doh-glee-fee-dah* f.
 toothpicks
οδοντοπαστα *oh-don-doh-
 pahs-tah* f. toothpaste
οδος *oh-dos* f. street, way
οινοπνευμα *ee-nop-nev-mah*
 n. alcohol
οκταποδι κρασατο *ok-tah-
 poh-dee krahs-sah-toh* see
 "National Dishes" p. 40 and
 "Regional Dishes" p. 52
οκταποδι με ρυζι *ok-tah-
 poh-dee meh ree-zee* see
 "National Dishes" p. 40
Οκτωβριος *ok-toh-vree-os* m.
 October
ολος *oh-los* pron. all
Ολυμπος *oh-lim-bos* see
 "Liqueurs" p. 28

ομελετα *oh-meh-leh-tah* f.
 omelette
ομως *oh-mos* conj. but
ονομα *oh-noh-mah* n. name
ονοματεπωνυμο *oh-noh-
 mah-teh-poh-nee-moh* n.
 name and surname
οξυγονο *ok-see-goh-noh* n.
 oxygen
ορεκτικα *oh-rek-tee-kah* pl.
 appetizers
ορεκτικο ποτο *oh-rek-tee-
 koh poh-toh* n. aperitif
ορεξη *oh-rek-see* f. appetite
ορτυκι *or-tee-kee* n. quail
ορτυκια πιλαφ *or-tee-kyah
 pee-laf* see "Regional
 Dishes" p. 57
οσπρια με μυδια *os-pree-ah
 meh mee-dyah* see
 "Regional Dishes" p. 56
οταν *oh-tahn* adv. when
ουλος *oo-los* n. gums
ουρανος *oo-rah-nos* m. sky
οφειλω *oh-fee-loh* v. to have
 a debt, to be indebted
οχι *oh-hee* adv. no

παγος *pah-gos* m. ice
παγωτο *pah-goh-toh* n.
 ice-cream
παιδακι *peh-dah-kee* n. child
παλαμιδα *pah-lah-mee-dah*
 f. swordfish

Παλινη *pah-lee-nee* see "Wines" p. 26

παντοπωλειο *pan-doh-poh-lee-oh* n. grocery store

παπια με μπαμιες *pah-pee-ah meh bah-mee-es* see "National Dishes" p. 40 and "Regional Dishes" p. 46

παπια ψητη *pah-pee-ah psee-tee* roast duck see "National Dishes" p. 40

παπουτσακια *pah-poot-sah-kyah* see "National Dishes" p. 40

παραγγελια *pah-rah-geh-lee-ah* f. to order (from a waiter)

Παρασκευη *pah-rah-skeh-vee* Friday

παρατεινω *pah-rah-tee-noh* v. to extend, to dilute

παστα παστιτσιο *pahs-tah pahs-steet-see-oh* f. pie

παστελια *pahs-teh-lyah* see "Sweets" p. 23

παστες *pahs-tes* see "Sweets" p. 23

παστιτσιο ολυμπου *pahs-steet-see-oh oh-leem-poo* see "Regional Dishes" p. 48

παστουρμας *pahs-toor-mahs* m. see "Sausages and Cold Cuts" p. 13 and "Regional Dishes" p. 44

Πασχα *pahs-kha* n. Easter

πατατα *pah-tah-tah* potato, τηγανητες *tee-gah-nee-tes* fried, φουρνου *foor-noo* baked

πατατες με αυγα *pah-tah-tes meh av-gah* see "Regional Dishes" p. 50

πατατες μουσακα *pah-tah-tes moos-sah-kah* see "National Dishes" p. 40

πατατες σε τουρτα *pah-tah-tes seh toor-tah* see "Regional Dishes" p. 50

πατατοκεφτεδες *pah-tah-toh-kef-teh-des* see "National Dishes" p. 40

πατσας *paht-sas* pork tripe , see "National Dishes" p. 40 and "Regional Dishes" pp. 46 and 52

παχυς *pah-hees* adj. fat

παω *pah-oh* v. to go

πεινα *pee-nah* f. hunger

πεπονι *peh-poh-nee* n. melon

περδικες κρασατες *per-dee-kes krahs-sah-tes* braised partridges, see "National Dishes" p. 41

περισσοτερο *peh-ree-soh-teh-roh* adv. more

πεστροφα *pes-troh-fah* f. trout

πευκο *pef-koh* n. pine

πεψη _pep-see_ f. digestion

πηλιον σπετσοφαϊ _pee-lee-on spet-soh-fah-ee_ see "Regional Dishes" p. 51

πιλαφ _pee-laf_ n. rice

Πινδος _pin-dos_ see "Wines" p. 26

πιπερι _pee-peh-ree_ n. pepper

πιπερια _pee-peh-ree-ah_ f. bell peppers

πιπεριες γεμιστες _pee-peh-ree-es yeh-mis-tes_ stuffed bell peppers, see "National Dishes" p. 41

πιπεριες τηγανητες _pee-peh-ree-es tee-gah-nee-tes_ fried bell peppers, see "National Dishes" p. 41

πιπεριες ψητες _pee-peh-ree-es psee-tes_ grilled bell peppers see "National Dishes" p. 41

πιρουνι _pee-roo-nee_ n. fork

πισω _pees-soh_ adv. behind, back

πιτα _pee-tah_ f. Greek pizza

πιτα με πρασα _pee-tah meh prahs-sah_ see "Regional Dishes" p. 49

πιτες για σουβλακια _pee-tes yah soov-lah-kyah_ f. see "Other Specialties" p. 30

πιτσα _peet-tsah_ f. pizza

πιτσουνια ψητα/φουρνου _peet-soo-nee-ah psee-_ _tah/foor-noo_ see "National Dishes" p. 41

πλατεια _plah-tee-ah_ f. plaza; audience

πλενω _pleh-noh_ v. to wash

πληροφορια _plee-roh-foh-ree-ah_ f. information

πληρωνω _plee-roh-noh_ v. to pay

πλοιο _plee-oh_ n. ship

ποικιλια γαρνιτουρες _pee-kee-lee-ah gar-nee-too-res_ pl. vegetables

ποικιλια ψαρια ψητα _pee-kee-lee-ah psah-ryah psee-tah_ see "Regional Dishes" p. 46

πολτος _pohl-tos_ m. mush

πομπαρι _pom-bah-ree_ see "Regional Dishes" p. 52

πορτοκαλαδα _por-toh-kah-lah-dah_ f. orangeade

πορτοκαλι _por-toh-kah-lee_ n. orange

ποσιμος _poss-ee-mos_ adj. drinkable

ποτε _poh-teh_ adv. never

ποτε _poh-teh_ adv. when?

ποτηρι _poh-tee-ree_ n. glass

ποτο _poh-toh_ n. liqueur

που _poo_ adv. where?

πουρες _poo-res_ m. purée

προβειος _proh-vee-os_ adj. ovines

προξενειο *proh-kseh-<u>nee</u>-oh* n. consulate

προφορα *proh-foh-<u>rah</u>* f. pronunciation

πρωι *proh-ee* n. morning

πρωινο *proh-ee-<u>noh</u>* n. breakfast

πρωτευουσα *proh-<u>teh</u>-voos-sah* f. capital

Πρωτοχρονια *pro-toh-hroh-nee-<u>ah</u>* f. New Year's Day

πως *pohs* adv. how?

ραδικι *rah-<u>dee</u>-kee* n. chicory

Ρακι *rah-<u>kee</u>* see "Liqueurs" p. 28

ραπανακι *rah-pah-<u>nah</u>-kee* n. radish (small)

ραπανακια σαλατα *rah-pah-<u>nah</u>-kyah sah-<u>lah</u>-tah* see "National Dishes" p. 41

ρεβιθι *re-<u>vee</u>-thee* n. chickpea

ρεγγα *<u>reh</u>-gah* f. herring

ρεστα *<u>res</u>-tah* pl. change (money)

ριγανη *<u>ree</u>-gah-nee* f. oregano

ριγανοκεφτεδες *ree-gah-noh-kef-<u>teh</u>-des* see "Regional Dishes" p. 48

ροδακινο *roh-<u>dah</u>-kee-noh* n. peach

Ροδιτις *roh-<u>dee</u>-tis* see "Wines" p. 26

ρυζι *<u>ree</u>-zee* n. rice

ρυζογαλο *ri-<u>zoh</u>-gah-loh* n. rice pudding see "Sweets" p. 23

ρωσικη σαλατα *ros-see-<u>kee</u> sah-<u>lah</u>-tah* f. Russian salad

Ρωσος *<u>ros</u>-sos* m. Russian

Σαββατο *<u>sah</u>-vah-toh* n. Saturday

Σαββατοκυριακο *sah-vah-toh-<u>kee</u>-ree-ah-koh* n. weekend

σαγανακι (στο) *sah-gah-<u>nah</u>-kee (stoh)* n. cooked in a pan

σαλαμι *sah-<u>lah</u>-mee* see "Sausages and Cold Cuts" p. 13

σαλαμια διαφορα *sah-<u>lah</u>-myah dee-<u>ah</u>-foh-rah* see "Regional Dishes" p. 44

σαλατα *sah-<u>lah</u>-tah* f. salad

σαλιγκαρι *sah-lee-<u>gah</u>-ree* n. snail

σαλιγκαρια στιφαδο *sah-lee-<u>gah</u>-ryah stee-<u>fah</u>-doh* snails with onions, see "National Dishes" p. 41

σαλτσα *<u>sal</u>-tsah* f. sauce

σαλτσα λαδολεμονο για λαχανο *<u>sal</u>-tsah lah-doh-<u>leh</u>-moh-noh yah <u>lah</u>-hah-*

noh see "Sauces and Condiments" p. 19

σαλτσα λαδολεμονο για ψαρια *sal-tsah lah-doh-leh-moh-noh yah psah-ryah* see "Sauces and Condiments" p. 19

σαλτσα με κυμα *sal-tsah meh kee-mah* see "Sauces and Condiments" p. 19

σαλτσα ντοματες *sal-tsah doh-mah-tes* see "Sauces and Condiments" p. 19

σαλτσα σαβορυ *sal-tsah sah-voh-ree* see "Sauces and Condiments" p. 19

σαμπανια *sam-pah-nyah* f. sparkling wine

σαρδελα *sar-deh-lah* f. sardine

σαρδελες λαδοριγανη *sar-deh-les lah-doh-ree-gah-nee* sardines with oregano, see "National Dishes" p. 41

σαρκεσαδα *sahr-keh-sah-dah* see "Regional Dishes" p. 52

σελινο *seh-lee-noh* n. celery

σελινοριζες με χοιρινο *seh-lee-noh-ri-zes meh hee-ree-noh* see "National Dishes" p. 41

Σεπτεμβριος *sep-tem-vree-os* September

σερβιτορος *ser-vee-toh-ros* m. waiter

σιναπι *see-nah-pee* n. mustard

σκαλτσουνια *skal-tsoo-nyah* see "Sweets" p. 23

σκαρα *skah-rah* f. grill

σκεψη *skep-see* f. thought

σκληρος *sklee-ros* adj. hard

σκορδαλια *skor-dah-lee-ah* see "Sauces and Condiments" p. 20

σκορδο *skor-doh* n. garlic

σοκολατα *soh-koh-lah-tah* f. chocolate

σοκολατακια *soh-koh-lah-tah-kyah* chocolates

σολωμος *soh-loh-mos* m. salmon

σουβλα *soov-lah* f. spit, skewer

σουβλακια *soov-lah-kyah* skewers of meat, see "National Dishes" p. 42

σουπα *soo-pah* f. soup

σουπια *soo-pee-ah* f. cuttlefish

σουπιες με σαλτσα *soo-pee-es meh sal-tsah*, cuttlefish in sauce see "National Dishes" p. 42

σουπιες τηγανητες *soo-pee-es tee-gah-nee-tes* see "National Dishes" p. 42

σουτζουκια *soo-zoo-kyah*

see "Sausages and Cold Cuts" p.14 and "Regional Dishes" pp 45 and 56

σοφριτο *sohf-reet-toh* see "Regional Dishes" p. 58

σπανακι *spah-nah-kee* n. spinach

σπανακοπιτα *spah-nah-koh-pee-tah* see "National Dishes" p. 42

σπανακοπιτες *spah-nah-koh-pee-tes* see "Regional Dishes" p. 55

σπανακορυζο *spah-nah-koh-ri-zoh* risotto with spinach, see "National Dishes" p. 42 and "Regional Dishes" p. 46

σπαραγγι *spah-rah-ghee* n. asparagus

σπιτικο *spee-tee-koh* n. house specialty

σπληναντερο στο φουρνο *splee-nahn-deh-roh stoh foor-no* see "Regional Dishes" p. 54

σπορακια *spoh-rah-kyah* see "Other Specialties" p. 30

στα καρβουνα *stah kar-voo-nah* f. barbecued

σταφιδα *stah-fee-dah* f. raisin, currants

σταφιδα κορινθιακη *stah-fee-dah koh-rin-thee-ah-kee* f. of Corinth grapes

σταφυλι *stah-fee-lee* n. grapes

στομα *stoh-mah* n. mouth

στρειδι *stree-dee* n. oyster

στρυφτη η κλωστοπιτα Θεσσαλιαs *strif-tee ee klos-toh-pee-tah thess-ah-lee-as* see "Regional Dishes" p. 48

συγνωμη *sig-noh-mee* f. excuse

συκο *see-koh* n. fig

συκωτακια τηγανητα *see-koh-tah-kyah tee-gah-nee-tah* fried slices of pig's liver, see "National Dishes" p. 42

συκωτακια ψητα σκαρας *see-koh-tah-kyah psee-tah skah-rahs* see "National Dishes" p. 42

συκωτι *see-koh-tee* n. liver

συναγριδα *see-nah-gree-dah* f. dentex

συναλλαγμα *see-nah-lahg-mah* n. exchange

συνταγη *sin-dah-yee* f. recipe

σχεδον *sheh-don* adv. almost

σχεδον ωμο *sheh-don oh-moh* n. rare (meat)

σωμα *soh-mah* n. body

ταβερνα *tah-ver-nah* f. tavern

ταμειο *tah-mee-oh* n. cashier

ταξιδι *tax-ee-dee* n. journey

ταραμας *tah-rah-mas* see "Other Specialties" p. 30

ταραμοσαλατα *tah-rah-mos-sah-lah-tah* see "Sauces and Condiments" p. 20

ταυτοτητα *tahf-toh-tee-tah* f. identity card

ταχινι *tah-hee-nee* see "Other Specialties" p. 30

ταχινοσουπα *tah-hee-noh-soo-pah* sesame seed soup, see "National Dishes" p. 42 and "Regional Dishes" p. 47

ταχυδρομειο *tah-hee-droh-mee-oh* n. mail

τελειος *teh-lee-os* adj. perfect

τελος *teh-los* n. fine

τελωνειο *teh-loh-nee-oh* n. Customs

τζατζικι *zah-zee-kee* see "Sauces and Condiments" p. 20 and "Recipes" p. 64

τηγανιζω *tee-gah-nee-zo* v. to fry

τηλεοπτικος *tee-leh-op-tee-kos* adj. television

τηλεοραση *tee-leh-oh-rahs-see* f. television

τηλεφωνημα *tee-leh-foh-nee-mah* n. phone call

τηλεφωνο *tee-leh-foh-noh* n. telephone

της ωρας *tis oh-ras* n. cooked

τι *tee* just pron. what?

τιμη *tee-mee* f. price

τιμοκαταλογος *tee-moh-kah-tah-loh-gos* m. price list

τιποτα *tee-poh-tah* pron. nothing

το *toh* art n. sing. the τα *tah* pl. the

τοννος *toh-nos* m. tunafish

τουρισμος *too-ris-mos* m. tourism

τουριστας *too-rees-tas* m. tourist

Τουρκος *toor-kos* m. Turk

τουρσι *toor-see* n. pickles

τραινο *treh-noh* n. train

τραπεζα *trah-peh-zah* f. bank

τραπεζι *trah-peh-zee* n. table

τραπεζομαντηλο *trah-peh-zoh-mahn-dee-loh* n. tablecloth

τραχανας *trah-hah-nahs* see "National Dishes" p. 42

τρ ιανταφυλλο γλυκο *tree-ahn-dah-fee-loh glee-koh* see "Regional Dishes" p. 56

τριτος *tree-tos* num. third, Τριτη *tree-tee* Tuesday

τροπος *troh-pohs* m. manner

τροφη *troh-fee* f. food

τροχονομος *troh-hoh-noh-mos* m. policeman

τρυγος _tree-gos_ m. grape harvest

τρωγω _troh-goh_ v. to eat

τσαϊ _tsah-ee_ n. tea

Τσαντάλη _tsahn-dah-lee_ see "Wines" p. 26

τσιπουρα _tsee-poo-rah_ f. gilthead

τσιρος _tsee-ros_ smoked anchovies, see "National Dishes" p. 43

τσχορβα σουπα _tshkor-vah soo-pah_ see "Regional Dishes" p. 52

τυρι _tee-ree_ n. cheese

τυροπιτα Ιωαννινων _tee-roh-pee-tah ee-oh-ah-nee-non_ see "Regional Dishes" p. 49

τυροπιτα Ρουμελιωτικη _tee-roh-pee-tah roo-meh-lee-oh-tee-kee_ see "Regional Dishes" p. 50

τυροπιτα Θρακικη _tee-roh-pee-tah thrah-kee-kee_ see "Regional Dishes" p. 45 and "Recipes" p. 65

τυροπιτακια _tee-roh-pee-tah-kyah_ pl. _feh-tah_ cheese filled pizza (folded and baked)

τωρα _toh-rah_ adv. hour

υγεια _ee-yee-ah_ f. health

υγιεινος _ee-yee-eenos_ adj. hygienic

υγρος _ee-gros_ adj. liquid, humid

υιος _yee-os_ m. son

Υμητος _ee-mee-tos_ see "Wines" p. 26

υπαρχω _ee-par-hoh_ v. to exist υπαρχει _ee-par-hee_ there is

υπερ _ee-per_ prefix super

υπνος _eep-nos_ m. sleep

υπογραφη _ee-poh-grah-fee_ f. signature

υστερα _ees-teh-rah_ adv. after, later

υψος _ip-sos_ n. height

φαβα σουπα _fah-vah soo-pah_ see "National Dishes" p. 43

φαγητο _fah-yee-toh_ n. dish, serving

φαγωσιμος _fah-gos-see-mos_ adj. edible

φακες _fah-kes_ see "National Dishes" p. 43

φαναρι _fah-nah-ree_ n. lamp, lantern

φαρμακειο _fahr-mah-kee-oh_ n. pharmacy

φαρμακο _fahr-mah-koh_ n. medicine

φασιανος _fahs-see-ah-nos_ m. pheasant

φασολαδα *fahs-soh-lah-dah*
f. bean soup see "National
Dishes" p. 42

φασολακι *fahs-soh-lah-kee*
n. beans (French)

φασολακια με κρεας *fahs-soh-lah-kyah meh kreh-ahs*
see "Regional Dishes" p. 54

Φεβρουαριος *fev-roo-ah-ree-os* February

φερνω *fer-noh* v. to bring

φετα τυρι *feh-tah tee-ree* feta
cheese, see "Cheeses" p. 16

φευγω *fev-goh* v. to go away

φιλετο *fee-leh-toh* n. fillet

φιλερι *fee-leh-ree* see
"Wines" p. 26

φιλια *fee-lee-ah* f. friendship

φιλοδωρημα *fee-loh-doh-ree-mah* n. tip

φιλοξενια *fee-loh-kseh-nee-ah* f. hospitality

φλιτζανι *flee-zah-nee* n. cup

φλογα *floh-gah* f. flame

φλουδα *floo-dah* f. skin, peel

φουντουκι *foon-doo-kee* n.
hazelnut

φουρνος *foor-nos* m. oven

ΦΠΑ *Ef.Pee.Ah* VAT

φραουλα *fra-oo-lah* f.
strawberry

φραπα *frah-pah* f. grapefruit

φραπε *frah-peh* milkshake

φρικασε *free-kahs-seh* see

"National Dishes" p. 43

Φρουταλια *froot-ah-lee-ah*
see "Regional Dishes" p. 51

φρουτο *froo-toh* n. fruit

φρουτοσαλατα *froo-toh-sah-lah-tah* f. fruit salad

φτηνος *ftee-nos* adj.
inexpensive

φυλλο για καταϊφι *feel-loh
yah kah-tah-ee-fee* see
"Other Specialties" p. 30

φυλλο για μπακλαβα η
καταϊφι *feel-loh yah bak-lah-vah ee kah-tah-ee-fee*
see "Other Specialties" p. 30

φυστικι *fis-tee-kee* n.
pistachio

φυστικι γλυκο του
κουταλιου *fis-tee-kee
glee-koh too koo-tah-lee-oo* see "Regional Dishes"
p. 56

φως *fos* n. light

φωτογραφια *foh-toh-grah-fee-ah* photography

χαβιαρι *hah-vee-ah-ree* n.
caviar

χαλβας *hal-vahs* see
"Sweets" p. 23

χαλβας θρακιωτικος *hal-vahs trah-kee-oh-tee-kos* see
"Regional Dishes" p. 45

χαλβας με σιμιγδαλι *hal-*

vahs meh see-mig-_dah_-lee
see "Sweets" p. 23 and
"Recipes" p. 70

χαλβας Φαρσαλων hal-_vahs_
far-_sah_-lon see "Regional
Dishes" p. 48

χαλουμι hah-_loo_-mee see
"Cheeses" p. 16

χαμογελο hah-_moh_-yeh-loh
n. smile

χαμομηλι hah-moh-_mee_-lee
n. camomile

χαπι _hah_-pee n. pill

χαρα hah-_rah_ f. joy

χαρη _hah_-ree f. favor

χαριτωμενος hah-ree-toh-
meh-nos adj. gracious,
sweet

χαρτης _har_-tis m. map

χαρτι har-_tee_ n. paper

χασαπικο has-_sah_ pee-koh
n. butcher's

χειρονομια hee-roh-noh-
mee-ah f. gesture

χελι _heh_-lee n. eel

χερι _heh_-ree n. hand

χηνα _hee_-nah f. goose

χθες hthes adv. yesterday

χιλιαρικο hee-lee-_ah_-ree-koh
a 1000-drachma bill

χλιαρος hlee-ah-_ros_ adj.
lukewarm

χοιρινο hee-ree-_noh_ pork

χοιρινο με σελινοριζα hee-

ree-_noh_ meh seh-lee-_noh_-ri-
zah see "Regional Dishes"
p. 47

χοιρομερι hee-roh-_meh_-ree
n. ham

χορευω hoh-_reh_-voh v. to
dance

χορος hoh-_ros_ m. dance

χορταρικα hor-tah-ree-_kah_
pl. vegetables

χορτατος hor-_tah_-tos adj.
satiated

χορτοσουπα hor-_toh_-soo-pah
f. minestrone soup

χορτοφαγος hor-toh-_fah_-gos
m. vegetarian menu

χουρμας hoor-_mahs_ m. date
tree

χρειαζομαι hree-_ah_-zoh-
meh v. to need χρειαζεται
hree-_ah_-seh-teh it's
necessary to

χρεωνω hreh-_oh_-noh v. to
debit

χρημα _hree_-mah n. money

χρηση _hrees_-see f. use

χρονος _hroh_-nos m. time, year

χρωμα _hroh_-mah n. color

χταποδι htah-_poh_-dee n.
polyp, octopus

χυμος hee-_mos_ m. juice

χωριατικη σαλατα hoh-ree-
_ah_-tee-kee sah-_lah_-tah
Greek salad

χωρις *hoh-<u>rees</u>* adv. without

χωρος *<u>hoh</u>-ros* m. space

ψαρεμα *<u>psah</u>-reh-mah* n. fishing

ψαρευω *psah-<u>reh</u>-voh* v. to fish

ψαρι *<u>psah</u>-ree* n. fish

Ψαρι πλακι *psah-ree plah-kee* see "Regional Dishes" p. 50 and p. 58

ψαρια τηγανητα *<u>psah</u>-ryah tee-gah-nee-<u>tah</u>* fried fish, see "Regional Dishes" p. 50

ψαρια φρεσκα *<u>psah</u>-ryah <u>fres</u>-kah,* fresh fish, see "National Dishes" p. 43

ψαρι χωριατικο *<u>psah</u>-ree hoh-ree-<u>ah</u>-tee-koh* see "Regional Dishes" p. 58

ψαρι παλαμιδα *<u>psah</u>-ree pah-lah-<u>mee</u>-dah* see "National Dishes" P. 43

ψαρι ροδιτικο *<u>psah</u>-ree roh-<u>dee</u>-tee-koh* f. see "Regional Dishes" p. 54

ψαροσουπα *psah-<u>roh</u>-soo-pah* f. fish soup

ψαχνο *psah-<u>noh</u>* n. pulp

ψαχνω *<u>psah</u>-noh* v. to seek, to search

ψησταρια *psis-tah-ree-<u>ah</u>* f. rotisserie, grill

ψητο *psee-<u>toh</u>* n. roast

ψυγειο *psee-<u>yee</u>-oh* n. refrigerator

ψυχη *psee-<u>hee</u>* f. soul

ψυχαρι *psee-<u>hah</u>-ree* living

ψωμι *psoh-<u>mee</u>* n. bread

ψωνια *psoh-<u>nyah</u>* pl. purchases

ωθω *oh-<u>thoh</u>* v. to push

ωκεανος *oh-keh-ah-<u>nos</u>* m. ocean

ωμος *oh-<u>mos</u>* adj. raw

ωρα *<u>oh</u>-rah* f. hour

ωραιος *<u>oh</u>-reh-os* adj. beautiful, handsome

ωραριο *oh-<u>rah</u>-ree-oh* n. timetable

ωριμος *<u>oh</u>-ree-mos* adj. ripe

ωσπου *<u>os</u>-poo* conj. until

ωστε *<u>os</u>-teh* conj. so that

ωστοσο *os-<u>tos</u>-soh* conj. however

ωφελουμαι *oh-feh-<u>loo</u>-meh* v. to benefit

ωχρος *oh-<u>ros</u>* adj. pale

INDEX

*Langenscheidt's Pocket Menu Readers
are also available for the following countries:*

France

Germany

Italy

Portugal & Brazil

Spain